KU-605-760

SCHOOLS IN SOCIETY

The evolution of English education

Eric Midwinter

BATSFORD ACADEMIC AND EDUCATIONAL LTD

© Eric Midwinter 1980

First published 1980
Printed in Great Britain by
Billing & Son Ltd
London, Guildford & Worcester
for the publishers
Batsford Academic and Educational Ltd
4 Fitzhardinge Street, London W1H 0AH

ISBN 0 7134 06585   (cased)
ISBN 0 7134 06593   (limp)

CONTENTS

LOCAL GOVERNMENT

THE TEACHING PROFESSION

3 EDUCATION AND THE SCHOOL

PRIMARY SCHOOLS

SECONDARY SCHOOLS

POST-SCHOOL EDUCATION

INTRODUCTION

Disraeli, a noted ignoramus in matters geographical, was asked by a lady at a social function the location of the Virgin Isles, at a time when those islands were political news. He didn't, he admitted, know, but he was sure they were as far as possible from the Isle of Man. One sometimes, sadly, feels that as broad a chasm separates the theory and practice of education. An age-old complaint by teachers is that an imbalance exists, and that their 'theoretical' training was weightier than their 'practical' instruction. Aspects of their studies, such as the development and organization of the educational system, are often recalled without affection. There may have been some interest; there was as frequently some boredom. But what has most bothered teachers has been the lack of connection between their academic exploration of such subjects and their day-to-day classroom preparation and practice.

This has, perhaps, been exacerbated by the business of mostly separating the academic studies of education and of subject disciplines from the more stressful experiences of actual classroom activity. It also reflects, truth to tell, some lack of capacity among teacher-students in making good their links themselves between the intellectual insights offered by academic study and the hectic hurly-burly of the classroom. Few would doubt that students for teaching need a unified and succinct backdrop of how the service they will work in came to pass and what its chief characteristics are, a backdrop, that is, against which to assess and improve their everyday labours. They need to place in social context and temporal perspective the issues which challenge and test them daily. By a grasp of the evolution and establishment of the chief factors in the teaching situation, it should be that much more possible for students and teachers to come to terms more effectively with such questions.

To that end, one has to look backward to the past, but the danger of lapsing into the merely antiquarian must be avoided. Teacher-tutors have, on occasion, not been blameless in face of the accusation that they have gazed back on education's story, sometimes examining it in heavy detail, without offering too many lines of inquiry or pragmatic assistance for teachers with a 40-year stint reaching into the next century. Similarly, there have been tutors who have inspected with students the current format of the system as if it had abruptly arrived, non-organic and administratively sterile, free from the impurities of years of political argument and other social features.

It is the contention here that the present British classroom, as the locale or site for a professional's working-life, has a present which was created in large part by its past and which offers a vantage-point to look critically a little into its future. One must, of course, recognize that it *is* a professional that one is discussing, which must surely mean someone going about his or her duties, not blindly, not automatically, not superficially, but with an intelligently constructive and in-depth understanding of the why's and wherefore's of these duties. It is not, therefore, a non-intellectual viewpoint, but rather a rigorously intellectual one, with day-by-day teaching practice judged constantly within its overall framework as built by historical, geographical, social, economic, political and a handful of other significant elements.

Here, then, is a small attempt to meet some of this exacting requirement. Here is an outline of the growth and present character of the public education service, with an increasing accent on the present and with an emphasis on what is useful to the serving teacher by way of comprehension of that public education service.

This book has been prepared after consultation with a group of working teacher-tutors, chosen on a nationwide basis. Almost without exception, they eschewed the traditional formula of a strictly chronological or overspecialized approach. They called for a thematic approach. They felt it was important for teachers to understand why the elements in their current teaching existence came about and what determined them. Otherwise, they believe, the students will become blinkered teachers, unaware of why and how they came to be operating in this or that manner, unable to focus or judge their work properly.

To meet this need, a three-fold plan has been adopted, with each part fitting into the previous one, like a series of playgroup boxes. Part 1—**Education and Society**—examines the overall context in which the education system has emerged and is operating, stressing the link between such national factors and the public education system. Part 2—**Education and the State**—relates to the political and administrative evolution of central and local control of education, and, alongside that, the establishment of the teaching force as a component of the state apparatus. Part 3—**Education and the School**—describes the growth and character of primary and secondary schools, and analyzes current issues concerning them, while touching briefly also on post-school education and the general problem of education and the community today. Each part, although not too rigidly so, is in sets of threes (often with the first one or two being precursors to a third which is an analysis of the related current issues), which may be taken together as a 'unit' of treatment. Thus the book tries to home in ever closer to the daily situation facing teachers, without ever losing sight of the elements which have determined that situation.

The outline of the book is deliberately simple and unshamedly geared to teacher-education either for pre-service training, both primary and secondary, or for in-service training in, for instance, the external B.Ed. degree. It assumes that most students are required to complete something in the order of a year's work on the development and present-day organization of public education. It assumes a normal three-term year, with some nine weeks of working time-table sessions in each term, and operates on the basis of a section or chapter each week. Obviously it is flexible enough to be open to other treatments, such as the more intensified 'unit' of, say, a term's length, or as a cross-check to other courses over a three or four year period. It is open for clear-cut use, therefore, on either the conventional timetable or in the most fashionable 'modular' approaches of today. In essence, the book is designed for seminar study. Each section or chapter is a link in the chain—but it is a 'link' which may be developed separately for group or individual study. Each topic, while logically a part of the sequence, is treated as an autonomous item for discussion and some suggestions for essays or seminar consideration have been added. Advice on further reading has also been included.

It is hoped that clarity of purpose and simplicity of outline has not made for too bland a book. Without deviating too far or too often from the straight and narrow path of objective and factual narrative, the author has not dodged a strongly personal, even sometimes controversial view, of the way education has grown and the manner in which it relates to society today. He has done so in the belief that too tame an account would scarcely stimulate lively discussion in seminar sessions nor heartfelt sentiments and views in essays. Overall, this is an attempt to enlighten teachers and students in their labours by placing these endeavours in their historical, social and organizational frame. As Winston Churchill astutely said, 'the use of recriminations about the past is to enforce effective action in the future'.

Dr Eric Midwinter

1 Education and Society

THE NATIONAL POLICY

1 THE HISTORICAL BACKGROUND TO MODERN SOCIETY

The English political invention of Parliamentary Government provided a propitious social setting for the subsequent English invention of Industrialism. 'Democracy' in the sense of a system of government in which the executive is responsible to a parliament which is representative of the people, and 'Industrialism' in the sense of a system of machine-production by 'hands' concentrated in factories, are the two master-institutions of our age. They have come to prevail because they offer the best possible solutions which our Western Society has been able to find for the problem of transposing the political and economic achievement of the Italian city-state culture from the city-state to the kingdom scale; and both these solutions have been worked out in England in the age of what one of her latter-day statesmen has called her 'splendid isolation'.

Arnold Toynbee *A Study of History* vol. iii (1933)

H. A. L. Fisher, minister in charge of the 1918 Education Act and author of a renowned history of Europe, said in his preface to that book: 'one intellectual excitement has, however, been denied me. Men wiser and more learned than I have discerned in history a plot, a rhythm, a predetermined pattern. These harmonies are concealed from me. I can see only one emergency following upon another as wave follows upon wave, only one great fact with respect to which, since it is unique, there can be no generalizations, only one safe rule for the historian; that he should recognize in the development of human destinies the play of the contingent and the unforeseen'.

This is a sagacious warning, and one carefully to be borne in mind by those attempting to throw some light on current issues by reference to past events. It is a necessary proviso, but not a prohibition. Granted the gross interplay of chance, there is still no gainsaying that, to understand and thus grapple with present-day matters in education or elsewhere, their origins and growth require some study. The system in which the teacher works has developed organically; it is a social process which, like an individual, a family or a nation, has evolved. The teacher who fails to recognize this is a blinkered teacher. To take the system as it stands for granted, as so many teachers disastrously do, is to teach with amnesia. The education service is not based on rational, logical blueprint; no tablets were handed down from Mount Sinai to such Mosaic figures as Mr Forster in 1870, Mr Fisher himself in 1918 or Mr Butler in 1944. The educational system is a mish-mash: the inchoate product of laws, individuals, ideas, architecture, social changes and Acts of God. To *assume* the system is to perpetuate it unknowingly: one must, to teach thoughtfully and efficiently, acquire a working grasp of how it came to be like this. One may accept it, or attempt to change it: either way the need to comprehend it is paramount. Educational history is littered with the remains of those who have tried to alter without understanding the growth pattern, of those who have intrepidly searched for the hissing gas leaks of education with the lighted matches of uninformed ideas.

When, for instance, you are invited to teach the life-cycle of the frog to a 'B' stream of 31 mixed children, who, at eight-plus, are in their second junior year at St Dunstan's Church of England (controlled) primary school in Division 12 of Loamshire local education authority, subject to inspection by the Department of Education and Science, in a classroom of 1,200 square feet, with steam-radiator heating, a central hall structure, an autonomously eccentric headteacher and a crate of gratis plastic cartons of milk in the corner of the room—you are faced with a dozen or more historical factors, all confronting you by dint of their formulation in the past.

Put another way, and while acknowledging the hazards of generalization, one must seek out some perspective so that the issues of the hour become more intelligible and, first of all, it is important to observe the character of the politico-economic context in which education occurs.

The country's education system is basically subjected to its confines within a nation-state. Overall sovereignty resides, for Great Britain, in its parliament and, eventually, all else is subordinate to that. This truism is worth stating because it is not, in historical terms, of especially long standing. The slow, ponderous construction of nationhood, perhaps reaching its apogee in the sixteenth century, replaced the old-style feudal kingdom with its much more pyramidal power-structure, so that, certainly by the time of the later Tudor monarchs, control rested firmly, never to be challenged, at the centre. This was accompanied by a massively increased commercialization of the economy; indeed many would regard this as the chief cause of the rise of the nation-state. Although medieval society had never enjoyed a completely agrarian and 'natural' economy, there was no denying that, in the modern state, money rather than land was the key to wealth. The inrush of gold from the new world—well over 2,000,000 kilograms in the 300 years after Columbus' epic voyage—and more systematic banking and coinage processes were part and parcel of this. The model for this new national economic unit was the older-style mercantile town with its strict commercial regulo. As Toynbee reminds, the Italian city state was the finest example.

Of course there were many other changes allied to these fundamental ones. A national religious accommodation, in the wake of the Protestant Reformation, the flowering of the national culture and literature as part of the Northern Renaissance, those remarkable technical innovations known as the Scientific Revolution, the growth of individualism and what loosely might be called a middle-class, and the development of a more thorough-going theory of statecraft—these were all associated with the move to modernism. But what was most compelling was the realpolitik of an omnicompetent nation-state with a money-economy. In Tudor England education came under the surveillance of the state. Apprenticeship—'the Englishman's School' in G. M. Trevelyan's splendid phrase—was controlled by such acts as the 1563 Statute of Artificers. The grammar school (and hardly any Tudor lad lived more than 12 miles from one) responded to new demands for commercial and administrative personnel, a notion properly and aptly expressed in Thomas Elyot's *The Governor*, published in 1531. Education was seen as one device for 'winning the West for Protestantism': there were supposed to be compulsory curriculum items of a politico-religious nature and teachers in Elizabeth's reign had to be registered and to vow in the 'Schoolmaster's Oath' allegiance to that spirited Queen.

Now there may have been modifications to that referential frame of a nation-state with a cash-nexus, but it has not, in Europe let alone Great Britain, been superseded. Multinational companies and trading alliances, such as the Common Market, may seem to sunder national boundaries, but the decision-making process remains sovereign to the state: indeed, the whole debate and action in regard to the European Economic Community has been founded on national self-interest. Thus the nation maintains its all but absolute rights over its citizens and they respond with what Arnold Toynbee, the historian of civilizations, has called the 'pagan deification of territorial blocs'. He has written of 'a divine right which is still working havoc in the Western World in the grim shape of a pagan worship of sovereign national states'. Patriotism, which Dr Johnson rather oddly described as 'the last refuge of a scoundrel' and which Nurse Cavell more discerningly declared to be 'not enough', has very largely superseded Christianity as the religion of the Western World.

We live and work today in 'this monstrous product of the impact of parochialism', but, over the last one or two hundred years, internal modifications have occurred. In chief, these have been two-fold. The political control of the nation-state by an absolute monarchy of the Tudor brand was replaced by a form of parliamentary or oligarchic governance. The Tudor monarchs, in truth, operated not autocratically but with an unwritten political contract with their well-to-do subjects, and it was the disintegration of this partnership that paved the route to parliamentary sovereignty. Alongside this, there has been the intense introduction of industrial technology as a major projection of commercialism, and this, like the advent of parliamentary democracy, has had significant effects. Nevertheless, each of these two pronounced changes occurred within the ambit of a 'national cash-nexus' society.

Within the confines of such a society, democracy and industrialism have continued to be the key determinants. From the first Parliamentary Reform Act of 1832 to the Universal Manhood Suffrage Act of 1928, the franchise was gradually widened to include all adults over 21, a provision latterly, of course, reduced to 18. This doctrine of the accountability of the executive to the people sharpened the development of party politics. By the last third of the century, the Conservative and Liberal Parties were the leading contenders for office, while, sometime after the First World War, the Labour Party replaced the latter as the alternate and slightly more radical government. None of these parties threatened the parliamentary machine as the essential prerequisite of national sovereignty, neither did any, incidentally, challenge in depth the rationale of the money economy.

What must be pressed, particularly from the viewpoint of educational administration, is that parliamentary government is 'representative' and not 'popular' democracy. In theory, the individual periodically leases his piece of political real estate, in both central and local government elections, and loses temporary control of his property rights. By way of illustration, the school is jointly administered in the final analysis by parliament and, by legislative devolution, the local education authority. Neither the teachers as the labour-force nor the parents and pupils, as the users of the service, can claim any day-by-day or popular authority over what technically is their public domain.

As for industrialism, its leading trait was the huge expansion of productivity, allied with the celebrated inventions of the age—in the 1760s, 12 patents a year was the norm, by the 1820s it was 250—and the coming of power-driven machinery. With coke-fired furnaces, Britain's production of iron sprang from 18,000 tons in 1740 to 2,500,000 tons in 1850, and that was half the world's production. One could pile example upon example. While France, our chief rival, had suffered the indignity first of revolutionary excesses and then ignominious defeat in the Napoleonic Wars, Britain had, conversely, enjoyed comparative peace on the home front and (the loss of the

American Colonies in 1783 apart) splendid martial successes abroad. All was set for a century in which Britain, the first European country to house both a parliamentary and an industrial system, was to be the premier world power, trading extensively and profitably and constructing a massive imperial connection. The peak was, approximately, the turn of the century. Thereafter the efforts of an evergrowing number of competitors, political and military as well as commercial, began to tell. Two world wars, cracks in the economic and financial mechanisms, the collapse of Empire: these have been the signs of exhaustion and decline, and thus contemporary Britain, overall, is, as E. J. Hobsbawn has said, 'a much more comfortable country to live in than ever before, a much more entertaining country, but also, from the historian's point of view, a much less important country'.

The effects of these democratic and industrial changes have very evidently transformed the social fabric of the nation and redrawn the social horizons of its people. Whether one turns to domestic comforts or public services for the yardstick, the improvement in material well-being of the people is beyond question. Whether one takes the number of television sets—there are close on 20,000,000 now in the country—or the number of holidays—something like 50,000,000 holidays, one in ten abroad, are taken annually—the issue of physical comforts is straightforward enough. A balance of technical progress, whatever its other disadvantages, with parliamentary oversight, whatever its other shortcomings, has ensured this.

Such a rise over the last hundred or so years in the nation's material stock had important remifications for education, not least because more people and more time and more funds were to become available. Equally important, however, and perhaps less overt, were the alterations in the social structure consequent upon the industrial/democratic revolution. The crucial characteristic of the newborn social system was what the historian Herman Finer has succinctly called 'congregation'. Britain was, relative to pre-industrial years, subject to a species of overcrowding, by which more and more people cramped themselves into more and more factories in evermore crowded towns. And those three sub-specimens of the species—the factory system, urbanization and the demographic explosion—were the critical features.

Like most historical processes, they interacted to the point where it is impossible to distinguish pure cause and effect. The widespread implementation of power-driven machinery, organized collectively meant, for instance, that spun-cotton production jumped from 1,000,000 pounds in 1741 to 22,000,000 pounds in 1787 and Manchester had 50 mills by 1800. In social terms, a wage-earning army was recruited to serve in the industrial barracks, were they mines, mills or foundries. This virtual setting of labour against capital, this confrontation of working- and middle-classes, had a series of effects, such as the rise of trade unionism. The factories in their turn were set in the towns, and, during the first half of the last century, many urban populations increased three and four-fold. Blackburn increased its pupulation by 500% to 65,000, while Bradford leapt from 13,000 to 104,000. In lesser degree, and for reasons social historians still argue over, the national population doubled in that same half-century. On a longer perspective, the demographic explosion was such that a population of 5,500,000 in 1800 had grown to 29,000,000 in 1900.

'Congregation' is a constant. Some 90% of today's population of something over 50,000,000 live in urban areas which occupy not much over 10% of the land, and industry is still emphatically factory-based. Possibly the most alarming aspect of 'congregation' was that it did—and does—pose age-old social issues in a fresh guise or from a fresh angle. The most desperate problems confronting any society revolve around the four social ills of ill-health, poverty, ignorance and lawlessness. These were, during the nineteenth century, propounded in 'congregational' form, with mass epidemics, like the 53,000 cases of cholera in 1849 alone, mass disorder and crime, with as many as 40,000 in 1839 living wholly by 'depredation', mass unemployment, as in Lancashire during the cotton famine of the American Civil War period, and mass ignorance, as illustrated by the fact that in many populous areas less than half those considered of school age were in attendance at schools. Unlike their Tudor forbears, early nineteenth-century rulers had judged it wiser to deploy their central powers frugally, but it soon became clear that these *laissez-faire* principles, so dear to the hearts of many Victorian politicoes and businessmen, were helpless against such catastrophic inroads. Interpreted as the economic dogma of 'free trade', they had not proved unsuccessful, but the sheer horror and anxiety produced by the social conditions of the nineteenth century forced governments toward collectivism, that is, considerably enlarged state interference. From the onset of the Victorian era in the 1830s and increasingly to the present day, the state, notably by highly centralized measures, has substantially intervened in what hitherto had been regarded as the private remit of the individual. Collectivism in response to 'congregation': there lies the administrative history of the United Kingdom over the last 150 years. One might measure this in terms of the proportion of income devoted to public rather than private expenditure, that is, via taxes and rates; or by the actual scope of daily life over which the state has assumed responsibility; or by the number of personnel employed by the state to cater for all its very many functions.

In a phrase, the state now presumes to accept responsibilities for matters which once were deemed to be the prerogative of the individual. To the degree to which welfare systems, nationalized utilities and other public services predominate, that is the extent to which the interests of the community, as represented by the state, are judged to take precedence over those of the individual. This collectivist proclivity is probably the most important historical theme in respect of education. This, simply, is the reason why children of the appropriate age are obliged to attend schools, the overwhelming majority of which are state-controlled and financed.

With, admittedly, not too much of a contribution from Fisher's 1918 Education Act, the construction of an evergrowing public education service as part of the collectivist response to the challenge of 'congregation' does provide some plot for what Fisher called 'the play of the contingent and unforeseen'. Set that minor drama (some might suggest tragi-comedy) on a stage built upon a national cash-nexus society, with the scenery denoting its parliamentary and industrial modifications, and one has a lay and approximate background against which to analyze the development and trends of English education today.

Essay subjects and seminar topics

1 'If the Police of the country were to be managed by the Home Secretary's department and if all the teachers of education in the country...were in the hands of the Government, a more despicable despotism would not exist'.

Mr Hadfield, MP for Sheffield, House of Commons 1856

These, and many other like possibilities have come to pass. Is our nation a 'despicable despotism' and if not, why not?

2 Conduct an inventory of the average classroom, fabric and contents. Now describe it denuded of all materials and items unavailable before 1870.

2 THE CASE FOR A PUBLIC EDUCATION SERVICE

My Lord,
I have received Her Majesty's Commands to make a communication to your Lordship on a subject of the greatest importance. Her Majesty has observed with deep concern the want of instruction which is still observable among the poorer classes of her subjects. All the inquiries which have been made show a deficiency in the general Education of the People which is not in accordance with the

character of a Civilised and Christian nation.

The reports of the Chaplains of Jails show that to a large number of unfortunate prisoners a knowledge of the fundamental truths of natural and revealed religion has never been imparted...

In all such instances, by combining moral training with general instruction, the young may be saved from the temptations to crime, and the whole community receive indisputable benefit.

Letter from the Home Secretary, Lord John Russell to Lord Lansdowne,
Lord President of the Council, establishing a Committee for Education 1839

In England and Wales today there is a huge industry. It costs (1978/79 figures) £8,000,000,000 a year to run it, and, as it is paid for out of public funds that means £160 a head, man, woman and child, every year. It employs 2,000,000 people, that amounts to one in ten of all those in employment in England and Wales. It has no less than 10,000,000 customers daily, and it has as many as 35,000 places of business.

It is, of course, the public education service. In 1833 a parliamentary bill, presented by the radical MP John Arthur Roebuck, for the organization of local committees to establish schools, was rejected, but a sum of £20,000 was made available to subsidize voluntary church schools. The National Society, which was Anglican, and the British and Foreign Society, which was chiefly non-conformist, were the principal beneficiaries as indeed they were the main sponsors of voluntary schools. The money was to be devoted to school buildings and the voting in a House of Commons Supply Debate was 50 to 26 in favour. The sum granted in the civil list to Prince Albert on his marriage to Victoria was £80,000. In 1839 a Committee of the Privy Council was set up by royal prerogative 'for the consideration of all matters affecting the education of the people' and 'to superintend the application of any sums voted by Parliament'. There was some excitement, presumably as it was realized that intervention was here to stay. A protest vote was lost by only 275 to 280 and the annual grant was agreed by the slender margin of but two votes.

In such an inauspicious and hesitant manner did the narrative of the public education service commence. In quantitative terms, its triumph has been colossal: even allowing for changing monetary values, a rise from £20,000 to £8,000,000,000 is astronomical. A prior reason for this astonishing success-tale was touched upon in the opening chapter in terms of collectivism combatting 'congregation'. But that predetermines a certain character in each of these contesting concepts. Part of the social evil of 'congregation' had to be perceived of as educational in nature and open to educative resolution; and collectivism had to have the wherewithal to provide an efficient set of public mechanics to put such a solution into practice. In essence the educational history of the last 140 years has been a counterpoise of those two themes.

Firstly, as to the social faults that education might remedy, the insistent justification at each stage of public educational investment has been that, economically and socially, the nation would stand to benefit. That must be emphasized. Although obeissance might be made to individual fulfilment, the crucial apologia for public spending has been the public good. In short, it is the stability and sustenance of the nation-state and its money economy, which is at stake. The justification is often couched in an admixture of those two socio-political and economic faces of the 'national cash-nexus' society. Thus the fear is often expressed that, without a further allocation of educational largesse, the internal security and/or the economic viability of the nation will somehow be damaged.

Consider the development of the English state education system. The conventional schedule is the familiar one referred to in the introduction, with educational history conveniently mapped by reference to legislative peaks.

a *1833:* As we have noted, inaugurated the period of state grants to voluntary schools, coupled with the protective device of an inspectorate.

b *1870:* The Education Act of that year introduced the School Board era, a phase when local committees could promote the first ever state schools 'to fill the gaps' left by the subsidized voluntaryist endeavour. In this period elementary schooling became, in practice, compulsory and free.

c *1902:* Next the 1902 Act established the national pattern of local education authorities which gave the country full and statutory coverage for elementary education and initiated the move towards improved secondary provision. The 1918 Education Act added to this by, for instance, requiring children to remain at school until they were 14.

d *1944:* But the 1902 reform effectively carried state education through to the famous 1944 Education Act which introduced secondary education for all, although, in the early post-war decades, this was maintained on a selective basis through the notorious 11-plus.

The 60s and 70s have, in their turn, marked the ascent of the comprehensive principle through the primary into the secondary schools (with the leaving-age lifted to 16), together with a large extension of post-school education.

Phase by phase, the number of persons undergoing longer and longer sessions of state educational provisions has grown and grown. The sheer quantities involved are perhaps the only non-contentious fact about the history of state education, and, each time the resources flowed, the sentiments proposed were the same. The first Secretary of the Privy Council Committee was Dr James Kay-Shuttleworth, one-time Assistant Poor Law Commissioner and author of *The Moral and Physical Condition of the Working Classes in Manchester (1832)*. 'The preservation of internal peace, not less than the improvements of our nation's institutions,' he opined, 'depends on the education of the working class...with pure religion and undefiled, flourish frugality, forethought and industry.'

In the famous peroration to his speech introducing the 1870 Act, W. E. Forster, (Vice-President of the Committee of the Privy Council on Education) exhorted the Commons in these words: 'upon this speedy provision of education depends also our national power. Civilized communities throughout the world are massing themselves together, each mass being measured by its force; and if we are to hold our position among men of our own race or among the nations of the world we must make up the smallness of our numbers by increasing the intellectual force of the individual.'

The 1895 Bryce Report on *Secondary Education* was the precursor to the 1902 Education Act. 'Not a few censors have dilated', the rport ended, 'upon the disadvantages from which young Englishmen suffer in industry and commerce owing to the superior preparation of their competitors in several countries of continental Europe. These disadvantages are real. But we attach no less importance to the faults of dullness and barrenness to which so many lives are condemned... Thus, it is not merely in the interest of the material prosperity and intellectual activity of the nation, but no less in that of its happiness and moral strength, that the extension and reorganization of Secondary Education seem entitled to a place among the first subjects with which social legislation ought to deal.'

It was, in 1918, H. A. L. Fisher's view of his own bill that its passage would tend to stimulate the civic spirit, to promote general culture and technical knowledge, and to diffuse a steadier judgement and a better-informed opinion through the whole body of the community. Some years later in 1926 the Hadow Report on the *Education of the Adolescent*, and a preparatory document for the 1944 Act, referred to 'the awakening and guiding of the practical intelligence, for the better and more skilled service of the community in all its multiple business and complex affairs...a country like ours, so highly industrialized, and so dependent upon the success of its industries, that it needs for it success, and even for its safety the best and most highly trained skills of its citizens'. And the 1943 White Paper on *Educational Reconstruction*, a preface to the 1944 Act, echoed these sentiments: 'In the youth of the nation we have our greatest national asset. Even on the basis of mere expediency, we cannot afford not to develop this asset to our greatest advantage.'

Finally, to complete this catalogue of social and economic rationalizations, the 1963 Newsom Report, *Half our Future*, claimed that schools must relate 'more directly to adult life, and especially by taking a proper account of vocational interests' and spoke of the need 'for a generally better educated and intelligently adaptable labour force to meet new demands'.

The hypothesis, in summary, is that a vocational element and a conformist element have combined in greater or lesser degree to press an accumulative case for increased public educational provision. Whether our masters' analysis has been correct and whether their investment has proved beneficial is not presently the issue. The fact is that the dangers they felt were inherent in an increasingly industrialized and democratized society and could, in their consideration, be dispelled in part by education. On the vocational side, preparation for the national economy—what the education historian, Brian Simon has called 'economic indoctrination'—has been the rule. On the conformist side, it is an effort to transmit the norms and values of society that its preservation might be guaranteed. The school is the nation's forcing-ground or bedding-out area for its own moral and social predilections. At its crudest, it is moral and cultural indoctrination: in Nazi Germany the kindergarten grace ran:

fold your little hands, bow your little head;
think of him who gives us, each our daily bread.
Adolf Hitler is his name;
Him we as our Saviour claim.

Frederick the Great said 'wie der Staat, so die Schule'; whatever the state is like, so will be the school. Whatever hazy notions may be promulgated about child development or individual realization, teachers should not forget that, at base, the state invests hugely in an education system to man its economy and sustain its civic fabric. It may never have been as extremist and clumsy as Adolf Hitler, but, from Lord John Russell onwards, the notion has been uppermost that the state could educate men to fit into the labour-market and adopt the traditional value-pattern.

So much for the rising tide of argument in favour of an ever increasing state schools service. The right-hand side of the equation concerned the ability of the state to provide such a service. That question might be simply examined in two parts. In the first place, such educational advances are impossible until the clientele and the resources are available. An educational programme is not, like food or clothing, an absolute necessity, and is thus reliant on the economy to produce sufficient margins of funds to sponsor it. Similarly, unless the prevailing economic system can afford to release some of its labour-force; that is, actually function without that fraction, an education service is futile. In the nineteenth century, children could not be released for education while the technical infrastructure of industry required their attention; when the technology was more sophisticated, they were, first, no longer needed, and, second, needed later but with educational skills. That uneasy balance between the economy and the school, part-trainer, part-custodian, is central to the relation of school and society.

In the second place, the nation had to be administratively geared to public intervention on the educational front. Parliament could whistle for a national system of schools, but, until managerial skills were aligned with those express needs, it could have remained an idle dream. Collectivism is heavily reliant on an elaborate bureaucratic methodology, and, over the years under review, devices such as the postal service, the typewriter and the telephone were to ease the way, although, of course, necessity would sometimes mother the invention of an administrative method. For instance, it is unlikely that the ubiquitous range of schooling inaugurated by the 1902 Act would have been possible without the local government reforms of 1888 which established the county councils.

The collectivist development of the public education system, therefore, can in large degree be described by reference to the current availability of resources and personnel on the one hand, and the state's current capacity for administrative action on the other.

Neither of these arguments—the 'preservationist' justification for public education and the organizational feasibility of its implementation—are exclusive. Human and political motives are seldom so singular. Over the last hundred years a myriad stimuli have urged politicians and educators to add more and more pieces to the educational system: religious and humane opinion, political and social expedients, devotion to particular causes, vested interests— academic and otherwise—a variegated host of motivations. The two rationales pressed here may not have been the sole factors, but they have been, at each stage in the evolution of the state educational system, the necessary factors. In that lies their critical import for the student of the present day teaching situation.

Essay subjects and seminar topics

1 Study in outline the education system of a nation or society different from England in time or place. To what extent does it

illustrate the tenet suggested in this chapter that education systems are primarily devised to secure the economic and civic regime of their host society?

2 Goethe claimed that, told of the military organization or legal system of a country, he could describe the country precisely. Do peoples also get the education service they deserve?

3 THE NATION TODAY

By almost any indicator Britain is a solid, healthy society, bursting with creative vigour. Its lack-lustre performance in what Blake called 'these dark, Satanic mills' is less a symptom of sickness than of health. Even in a difficult year like 1974, a government census found that 84.4% of all men workers pronounced themselves as 'satisfied' with their jobs; for women, the rate was 89.4%. This is not the response of a sullen, class-ridden, divided nation.

The Press, both domestic and international, is vocationally compelled to take a short-term view of events and seize on crisis, real or imagined. This craft compulsion accounts for much of the lopsided image broadcast by the media. With an inflation rate above its industrial homologues, an unemployment level close to the highest tides elsewhere in the West, with growing hostility between jobless whites and black and brown immigrants, Britain is hardly the New Jerusalem. Neither is it the sinking, chaotic, miserable swamp depicted by the more imaginative journalists and professors. When and if stagflation is overcome throughout the West, Britain's preference for leisure over goods may yet serve as a model for others in the post industrial age.

Bernard Nossiter *Britain: A Future That Works* (1978)
London Correspondent of the *Washington Post*

It has been said that if goldfish were anthropologists, the last thing they would discover would be water. It is certainly not easy to stare one's own society full in the face and comprehend it entirely For example, one tends to notice the differences, either with the same society in the past or other societies at present. Social history often proffers more of a monotone, a series of variations on similar themes. The British nation-state, like most others in the world, whatever their overt political persuasion, is a corporate state, massively centralized. Where elements of its economic life remain in private hands, these are dominantly in the thrall of large, sometimes supranational, companies. From the direct viewpoint of the man in the street, the distinction between, say, the National Coal Board—a public utility—and the Imperial Chemical Industries—a technically private company, but one very involved with governmental planning and financing—is academic. In most of their day-to-day dealings the ordinary individual finds himself in negotiation with 'institutions'. be they public or private. His work may be of this kind; his shop may be part of a long supermarket chain; his newspaper may be published by a mammoth combine; his house financed by a large-scale building society; his television programmes produced by either a huge state or a huge commercial agency, and so on.

The 'superstructure' of our society is obvious enough. The warts and all are there for everyone to see: the fact that we have sliced bread and double-glazing now whereas our grandparents didn't, or the fact that we have less murders than the USA or more cricket than France. It is equally evident that our place in the world political and economic league has slipped since the Second World War, and that, with our Empire disintegrated and our economy somewhat outmoded, Britain is a second-class power.

From the teacher's stance, however, the nature of the 'structure' of society is probably more important to grasp. Jeremiahs about the British economy and British morale may be convincing enough, but they are assuredly no novelty—groans about the frailties of either can be traced back into the sixteenth century. Indeed, and for the majority of children teachers are likely to meet, the one constant about progress is the amelioration of material circumstances over the last hundred years. The health, nutrition and general physical treatment of children has undoubtedly improved.

The present-day corporate state must take some of the credit for this. Whatever its defects, it has contrived to organize a stupendously great increase in the national commonwealth and to distribute the proceeds a little more evenly. Whether the price—spiritually, morally—has made for a fair bargain is debatable; the fact of a monster bureaucracy controlling a complex set of mechanics yielding higher levels of localized domestic contentments, is not.

It is not surprising, then, that the rise of the public education service, briefly sketched out in the previous chapter, was not accomplished in a vacuum. As the state grew more collectivist, more corporate, so did the education system grow—and it is a process noticeable in most other European countries on either side of the Iron Curtain. Further, the main bounds ahead towards corporatism have each tended to be typified by an appropriate spring forward in the education system's evolution, as the following description, using the scheme adopted in the previous chapter, reveals.

a *The 1830s:* When the first state grants, state inspectors and state committee of the modern era were introduced, was a time of general administrative reform—the first Parliamentary Reform Act (which, roughly speaking, enfranchised the middle class), the reform of the poor law system, the reform of town government in the Municipal Corporations Act, some early attempts at police reform, a certain amount of factory legislation, to name but five examples. Without the 1836 Act for the Registration of Births, Deaths and Marriages, future attempts to administer schemes like public elementary schooling for all would have been severely incommoded, even if possible. Such legislation was chiefly furthered by the radical Whig Ministry of Lord Grey and his colleagues.

b *The 1870s:* Following the second Parliamentary Reform Act of 1867, which gave the vote to the urban worker, there came the mighty administration of Gladstone's first Liberal government. Along with Forster's 1870 Education Act, which allowed for the installation of local school boards with rights of rate-levying for the erection and upkeep of schools, there was a plethora of administrative reforms. The Army, the Civil Service the prisons, the Licensing Laws, the Trades Unions—these were some of the great national institutions which felt the heat of Gladstone's demonic reforming zeal. As his cabinet faced defeat, his arch-rival Disraeli described the Liberal front bench, half-scornfully, half-admiringly, as 'a row of extinct volcanoes'. Disraeli himself then furthered these early and quasi-collectivist changes with his own social legislation, notably with the seminal Public Health Act of 1875.

c *The 1900s:* Again it was a Liberal government which, coming to power in 1906, indulged in several measures of social intervention, including the first old age pensions, employment insurance and other welfare legislation. Asquith, Lloyd-George and Winston Churchill were the names to conjure with in this administration, but it was preceded by Balfour's 1902 Education Act, a Conservative statute which, by deployment of the County Councils,gave England and Wales uniform educational management. The First World War, pressing close on this reform programme, added considerably to the number of regulations and controls to which citizens were subjected, and, in 1918, Fisher's Education Act was passed.

d *The 1940s:* This time a war—the Second World War—came first, involving as it did a massive intervention by the state on the privacy of the individual. Rationing and conscription are two instances, but it has been calculated that, between the declaration of war and 1943, the number of civil servants doubled to 700,000.

The 1944 Education Act, which provided for secondary education for all and inaugurated a period of phenomenal growth in the education system, was the prelude to the so-called 'silent revolution' of Clement Attlee's 1945-51 Labour Ministry. The nationalization of public utilities, like gas, railways and coal, coupled with the co-ordination of social protection into the cradle-to-grave cover of the welfare state, with the National Health Service (founded in 1948) at its hub, more or less ended the creation of the modern state.

These periods form pools of emphasis. Between-times there were phases of legislative quiescence. This does not mean that they included no statutory encroachment by the state, merely that, relatively speaking and for whatever reasons of political philosophy or practice, the action was less brisk. What of the last 30 years? Despite two spells of purportedly social democratic Labour Governments (1964-70 and 1974-79), one would be hard put to point out any major items of collectivist legislation. Compared with the reform of the army or the 1875 Public Health Act or the introduction of health insurance or the establishment of the National Health Service, most recent endeavours in such fields have looked decidedly puny. Successive governments have managed the economy and the social system, tinkering and adjusting both with whatever tools and skills were to hand, but scarcely ever hazarding wholesale reform. The important reforms of the age—on divorce, abortion, homosexuality, capital punishment—have tended to be individualist rather than collectivist. Of course it might be that the state's maw is chock full, that the process of centralism has by now become so far advanced that there is little else left to encompass.

And, although largescale alterations in the body politic have not featured in the parliamentary life of the last 30 years, governmental action has continued to be weighty. Partly through fiscal controls but also by statutory enactment (as in the case of the Labour government's insistence on the comprehensive mode of secondary schooling) the Department of Education and Science has, in the opinion of most commentators, grown remarkably powerful over the last score or so years.

So the general expansion of the corporate state has encompassed a similar rate of increase in the educational system. The proportion of daily life taken up by the public sector is reflected in the size of the budget, national and local, required to man it. Similarly with education. It costs £15,000,000 a week, and, for example, the Oxfordshire lea (local educational authority) employs more personnel than British Oxygen in Oxfordshire.

This reversal of the state-individual balance, has from, say, the 1830s been quite dramatic. When, in Victorian England, it was believed that four in a 100 of London's females were prostitutes and perhaps some action was called for, a *laissez-faire* enthusiast thundered: 'we may by no reason deprive the female of the right to abandon herself privately for love, lust or lucre'.

Now our day is spent mostly in the public maw. Having awoken in, for a third of us, a council-owned house, warmed and lit by a nationalized industry (and having checked our watches by the public broadcasting corporation's time signal) we blearily fill our kettle from the public water supply before heating it with one or another of the state energy authority's devices, the while urging our children to gird up their loins for a day in the state school, as we flip through our state-delivered mail, much of it, using myself as a limited sample, from public bodies, e.g. the inland revenue.

Out then, onto the local authority's pavement and roadway, leaving our dustbin to be emptied by that same august institution, as we proceed often via public transport, to work which, for one quarter of us, is in the public sector. Wearily we will return home through streets lit and policed by the public authority, pausing only to admire the brave lads of the public-owned fire or ambulance service as they venture forth on some errand of mercy. Luckily, we may not have needed the health service, the social security set-up or the law courts, to say nothing of the army, navy and air force, during our normal working-day, but we may care to drop in at our local authority leisure centre, park, swimming pool or library as the mood suggests.

We are creatures of the corporate state. The bill for all this in 1975 was over £54,000 m., a tab picked up in rates, taxes, direct and indirect, and so forth. The people pay: the people use. It is a cradle to grave process. It is rather chilling to recall that the hands which bring us, mewling and puking, into this largely non-private society are those of a state-employed midwife, and, when faced with the ultimate in consumer choices, it will be the municipal crematorium which will complete our shuffling off this public coil.

This is not the direct consequence of Socialist endeavours, although Socialist theories and campaigns have played their part. A similar trend towards corporateness is discernible in most other countries, almost as if this is a *sine qua non* of the technically developed economy. Bismark introduced old age pensions into Germany years before they were envisaged here, while the comparisons between the American-based corporation and the Russian state-corporation are clear enough. The impact on education of a technologically advanced economy and a correspondingly intricate bureaucracy has been enormous. It makes a public education service necessary and possible, but it also shapes its content and ethos. The special employment needs of a heavily technical and bureaucratic nation-state do, or should, effect the nature of education's substance, while the cultural changes subsequent on high technology—television, increased leisure—also have a marked effect.

The atmosphere in which the school operates is thus of a different order. Relative affluence and a weighty officialdom have led, it would appear, to a loosening of the conventions and disciplines of the traditional mould. Comparative consumer satisfactions and the distancing effects of large-scale institutions have meant an implicit challenge to authoritarian values. This is for good or ill, dependent on one's moral and political predilections. Some point to the wholesome and life-enhancing quality of such freedoms; others to vandalism, violent crime and hooliganism. Certainly social problems are never solved; they are merely rewritten in terms of current contexts. Thus poverty is redefined in a connotation of urban blight or ill-health in a connotation of modern stress. In that 'education' is the response to 'ignorance', this, too, has fresh outlines, and questions of curriculum, of standards, of discipline, indeed of all the issues which have always faced teachers are sharply raised.

Needless to say, the economy has its sombre downs as well as its cheery ups, and political questions like devolution or the Common Market must not be discounted. In the broad span, however, of a teacher's 40 years' career, these tend to even out, and it is difficult to envisage a mid-term future which is not of a technocratic and corporate character. Something of the same applies to social relationships. Affluence, welfarism, technology and institutionalism doubtless alter the nature of the social classes, but the changes are most likely of degree rather than kind. The old-style middle-class is now composed more of managers, executives, officials and professionals, to the point where some sociologists have labelled it 'the service class'. But, however blurred the borderlines, Britain remains a class-society, in the sense that membership of socio-economic categories confers more or less distinct advantages or disadvantages, not least on the educational front. Here again, Britain is not unlike its neighbours overseas whether they rejoice under the flags of freedom or the banners of communism: varying groups of haves and have-nots may be discerned in each nation, their socio-economic position determining their particular package of life-chances.

The more we change. . . . The sixteenth-century Spanish Empire was described by a shrewd English observer as 'a Colossus stuffed with clouts', and some may wonder whether that appellation might not be as aptly applied to our frighteningly large techno-bureaucracy. Although at times it may seem far away from the teaching of reading to infants or the vicissitudes of the biology 'O' level class, it is emphatically the omnipotent presence in every classroom and in every school.

Essay titles and seminar topics

1 'The accumulation of material possessions is no compensation for the rupture between the individual and society that is

characteristic of competitive society'. (Aneurin Bevan, 1952). Discuss.

2 'Giants stamping on pygmies is the characteristic pattern of the age.' (George Orwell, 1944). How accurate do you think this perception of British society is today?

EDUCATIONAL THOUGHT AND CULTURE

4 THE EDUCATION DEBATE

The more young Joe submitted, the more absolute old John became ... old John was compelled to these exercises of authority by the applause and admiration of his Maypole cronies, who, in the intervals of their nightly pipes and pots, would shake their heads and say that Mr Willet was a father of the good old English sort; that there were no new-fangled notions or modern ways about him; that he put them in mind of what their fathers were when they were boys; that there was no mistake about him; that it would be well for the country if there were more like him, and more was the pity that there were not. . . . Then they would condescendingly give Joe to understand that it was all for his own good, and he would be thankful for it one day

Charles Dickens *Barnaby Rudge* (1841)

Old John Willet, landlord of the Maypole Inn, Chigwell, about 1785, serves for all time as a 'father of the good old English sort'. From much earlier than Georgian England to the *Black Papers* of the modern era, the knell is sounded that children are less well-behaved and less well-educated than their immediate forbears, and that the fault lies with 'new-fangled notions or modern ways'. Indeed, were each succeeding generation to have been accurate in its analysis, the nation would have been sunk without trace and years ago in a morass of anarchic illiteracy. One would be much pressed to find fathers saying to their sons: 'in our day things were much softer and easier, and standards were lower'.

The gloomy retrospect is a constant in the educational debate, and teachers must beware it, not only in society but in themselves. The senior teacher, horrified by the polo-necked sweater and jeans of the young male or the trousers of the young female of the species, has forgotten how risqué it had been in his turn to wear sports jacket and flannels among colleagues suited and gowned. This is not the prelude to a paean of progress. Education, like any other social progress, does not automatically improve. There may be shifts in achievement, some of them due to inefficient new methods, but, overall, the likelier scenario is one of swings and roundabouts.

Heraclitus pointed out that 'man steps but once in the same river', so that 'standards', as absolutes, soon become slippery commodities. Standards have to be set against the changing river. Arguably, literacy was of less social and economic value 300 years ago — and, after a century or so in the ascendant, the audio-visual and computerized techniques of the future make it of comparatively less value once more. The argument about reading levels which has raged through the 1970s has been a classic of its kind. On the one side, there has been controversy about the actualities of literacy. The progressives claimed that reading has improved considerably since the war, while their opponents pressed the reverse view. Industrialists complained that young clerks could not spell, and educational administrators retorted that the job market had altered, so that the clerks of yesteryear were going on to college and a lower grade of clerks was issuing forth. It was further argued that 'informal' methods in the primary school and an end to selection in the secondary sector had led to deplorable academic results. Proponents of these methods claimed that there was an improvement in attainment because of them, and pointed to an increase in the numbers of the age-group getting five 'O' levels from 15% to 23% from mid-60s to mid-70s, and to the fact that those obtaining at least one 'A' level nearly doubled (9% to 16%) in the same period. Back came the riposte: 'O' and 'A' level standards themselves had dropped alarmingly.

Some of the same difficulty shrouds arguments about method. The authors of the *Black Papers* were keen to denigrate so-called 'modern' methods for poor results, but surveys were to suggest, in the late 70s, that many fewer schools had adopted them than popular lore foretold. Blame, if blame were justified, had to be laid at the old school-house door of the three 'R's. Thus, as well as ensuring that the facts are reasonably safe, observers of the debate must also determine the standpoint of the debaters.

For the young teacher facing forward into a profession where, paradoxically, many judgements are taken backwards, it is comfort, chilled but nonetheless comfort, to recognize the perpetual nature of the rows. The consistent element, over the last hundred or so years, has been the fairly rapid increase in the sheer quantity of education, but, in terms of a general educational debate, this has served only to change the milieu for the same cast of discussion. In the late nineteenth century Friedrich Nietzsche said: 'higher education and greater numbers—that is a contradiction in terms', and this might serve as a text for one stream of the debate.

As early as 1723 Bernard Mandeville was attacking the notion of increased education. He ridiculed the Charity Schools of his time which were attempting to spread literacy and the Christian doctrine among the lower orders. He appended his *Essay on Charity and Charity Schools* and his *A Search into the Nature of Society* to his famous *The Fable of the Bees; or Private Vices, Publick Benefits* (originally published nine years earlier). 'The more,' he said, 'a shepherd or ploughman know of the world, the less fitted he'll be to go through the fatigue and hardship of it with cheerfulness and equanimity'. And 'Charity-Schools, and everything else that promotes idleness and keeps the poor from working are more accessory to the Growth of Villainy, than the want of Reading and Writing.'

The view that overmuch education for too many people is wrong still continues to find favour, although, as the age-range for public provision has risen, so has the angle of the debate. In the 60s, for instance, the terse phrase, associated with Kingsley Amis and others, of 'more means worse' was coined to fault the annual influx of students into higher education from about 220,000 to over 430,000 over the decade. It is interesting to note that the argument about selection keeps pace with that about quantity and quality. Elementary education for the lower classes, as opposed to a superior form for the upper classes, slowly vanished into what might be called the 'comprehensive' primary school somewhere after the turn of the century.

The limelight was then turned on to the secondary education, available chiefly to the well-to-do. As it was made more uniform of access, modes of selection—the scholarship exam, the 11-plus—were built into the process, until, in the late 50s and 60s, the mood became favourable towards comprehension. This occurred at much the same time that, in its turn, higher education, traditionally the preserve of the well-heeled, was becoming more available and more highly selective. Now, with talk of a recurrent or lifelong educational system, educationalists like Robin Pedley argue for an open-ended or comprehensive higher education service.

The anxiety over the amount of education available is naturally related to another strand in the age-old discussion, namely, is it, from society's viewpoint, for better or for worse? This is now normally elaborated on the two features of modern life pinpointed in chapter 2, industry and democracy, or the economic and social poles of national stability. The belief that education is a prerequisite of politico-economic security is widespread and apolitical. One of the earliest modern experiments in state education was in Prussia in the 1790s, a Prussia hammered into submission and humiliation by the armies of Napoleon, a Prussia seeking desperately for survival. King

Frederick William III wrote to his chief minister, Baron von Stein: 'Our state has lost much in external power and splendour, but that is all the more reason why we should direct our attention towards winning for it an internal power and splendour. It is my formal desire that the most minute attention be given to popular instruction.' By 1819 Prussia was able to promulgate its famed Law of Public Instruction, with the University of Berlin at the fulcrum of one of Europe's first complete systems of public schooling, and with the educational teachings of Pestalozzi as its ideal. Equally, and at much the same time and at the opposite extreme of the political spectrum, the United States of America was making the same assumption. If a single nation was to be created from a divergent mix of religions and races, and one itself faced with an urgent and mammoth task of internal colonization westward to the Pacific, then the common school was necessary to enable children to absorb a common language and a common set of values. Now, with 90% of its youth not leaving school until 18 and over a third continuing beyond that age, the United States has certainly acted in the knowledge that education is essential to a highly industrialized and democratized society.

Conversely, this view has always been strongly challenged, and from both the standpoints of political sustenance and economic maintenance. In Victorian England the debate continued as to whether, in the words of the student howler, 'the peasants would be more or less revolting' if they could read and cypher. The view of Lord John Russell and Kay-Shuttleworth that literacy would lead to a wider acceptance of religious truth and thereby civil and economic order was pooh-poohed by many.

That fear of over-education is not dead. The seditious potential of education is reflected in the view of businessmen that informal or discovery methods produce too much questioning an attitude among those required to toe the production line of the factory in the disciplined manner. Religious education's place is often defended on the grounds that it preserves the traditional values, just as the castigation of far-left politically motivated teachers, real or imagined, stems from a belief that too unrestrained a schooling could be damaging.

The feeling many had and have that too much education might rock the boat politically, is also to be found in the world of commerce. Here the line is that education is not vocational enough. Either it does not teach would-be typists to spell correctly, or, by its passion for the liberal arts, it diverts attention from the sober but necessary business of engineering. The 'Great Educational Debate' of 1977/78, launched by James Callaghan, when Prime Minister, was motivated—and its content dominated—by the notion that education was somehow letting the economy down, and that the nation was not receiving sufficient benefit from its investment.

But this aspect of the debate taps deeper veins of analysis. It is convincingly pressed by some commentators that we have the equation reversed. It is not that, as the Robbins Report 1963 intimated, 'the communities that have paid most attention to higher studies have in general been the most obviously progressive in respect of income and wealth', but that an advanced economy permits the luxury of an advanced educational system. In the words of E. G. West, most trenchant and fluent of Britain's critics of a collectivist education system: 'a high educational expenditure correlated with a high GNP may be an effect rather than a cause of prosperity in the same way that a millionaire's Cadillac is evidence not of the means of making his fortune but of his enjoyment in the consumption of it'. West quotes the instance of Lyon Playfair, the Victorian chemist, ascribing Belgian and German prowess in industry in the late nineteenth century to superior scientific education — an opinion which led to increased state support for technical and scientific education in this country. Recent investigations, in West's view, demonstrate that it was changing market opportunities and legal inihibitions, not lack of skills, which caused the Belgian and German advance.

The argument about whether and to what extent education should be provided by the state is, therefore, a complicated one, and it is not as straightforward as, at first sight, it appears. When a teacher is faced with a group of children, their immediate care and nurture will be uppermost in the professional mind. It is too easy, in that situation, to take on trust, to take for granted, the valid existence of a great state institution. Eventually, however, the objectives and justifications for widescale public provision must impinge on the daily life of teacher and pupils; are you preparing them for a job and useful citizenhood, or are you keen to turn out bright and bushy-tailed individuals, knowledgeable and alive for the sake of knowledge and life? Many teachers would, if pressed, admit to seeking for a balance between the public good and self-realization, if only in terms of the boy with two 'A' levels obtaining a more satisfactory and better-paid occupation, with his happy lot contributing to the national good.

That the appropriate pastiche of neo-Benthamism may not, in fact command wide professional support. The Schools Council's *Enquiry 1, Young School Leavers* showed that the majority of teachers 'rejected the achievement of vocational success as a major objective of education', preferring to develop 'the characters and personalities of pupils, to teach them ethical values and to help them become mature, confident and successful in their personal relationships'. Conversely, parents and pupils were most interested in 'the provision of knowledge and skills which would enable young people to obtain the best jobs and careers of which they were capable'.

This implicit chasm between what society, as represented by parents and school-leavers, anticipates from the education service and what teachers regard as its prior function illustrates, at the mundane level of the classroom, how complex a philosophic issue this is. And a final dimension must be added, and one that will be returned to in further chapters. This is the gigantic poser about the potency of the school as a change-agent. Granted that some accommodation could be found for parents wanting an instruction for industry and teachers wanting an instruction, in its broader terms, for democracy, may we be sure, whatever resources we pour into the schools, that they are capable of creating or maintaining such positions? Were the governments of Prussia and the United States right to presume that schools could produce the sought outcome of national unity and power, or did Prussia, later Germany, and the United States emerge as significant modern powers in spite of large-scale popular education? Would our own industrial needs and democratic aspirations falter, remain steady or soar according to dramatic ascents or descents in educational investment?

The educational debate, like most others, continues.

Essay subjects and seminar topics

1 'Modern education has devoted itself to the teaching of impudence, and then we complain we can no more manage our mobs'.

John Ruskin (1819-1900)

Is this eminently Victorian opinion more or less applicable today? For instance are 'creative' methods conducive to 'impudence', and is this an advantage or a disadvantage for society?

2 '(higher education) is, on the whole, a bad training for the real world and only men of very strong character surmount this handicap.'

Paul Chambers, I.C.I. Chairman 1964

An industrialist's view of the intellectual versus the pragmatic contest in education. Which side seems to be winning the tug-o'-war at present; and which side would you support?

5 THE SOCIAL AND CULTURAL FABRIC

Back home, Jane can now spare an hour for her new book on the international monetary system, She is in the middle of a chapter on the consequences of the British decision to close the Mint within five years, now that virtually all transactions are cashless.

Jane is a traditionalist. She likes to see the words as she writes. Therefore the desktop computer in her study has an antique keyboard with letters. As she types, the words appear on the screen before her. The computer corrects her spelling and, on its irritating days, argues with her about grammar and punctuation.

Few people are still prepared to bother with the discipline of the keyboard; they dictate their letters and instructions to the machine and let it get on with them.

At least, the twins, aged eight, seem to have exhausted their propaganda campaign for a more chatty teaching robot than their tiny model. But that thought only recalls to Jane's mind the sole area of marital dispute: education.

Jane and Joe's job categories mean that they can get exemption from sending the children to the reopened village school: it is assumed that they will ensure that the twins follow the appropriate syllabuses of the national school TV network, which includes an interactive (talking back) element.

Jane hankers for the old, direct encouragement of the personal teacher of her school and university days. Joe accepts the orthodox theory that is now applied in almost all professions: it is better to use the skills of the most gifted individuals for the benefit of all — whether the required advice is medical, legal, horticultural, or whatever.

Peter Large, *The Guardian* 17th February 1979

Although the parameters for provision of education may ever be determined by and for the long-term factors of economics and politics as outlined in previous chapters, slight shifts in the politico-economic cosmos do produce stellar movements. In education they appertain, in chief, to cultural and social questions. For instance, an advanced technology has not only invented television but made it accessible to all, and that has important consequences for education. Let us take television and examine it as an instance of one such piece of cultural and social revision. It is not the only cultural change of the last 50 years, and some would say it was not the most significant. Nonetheless, and without altering any of the basic tenets of schools and their link with society, it is, at worst, intrusive, and may vividly serve, *pro tem.*, as a model of this category of internal changes of educational circumstances.

The possible effects of television are fourfold. In the first place, it offers a helpmeet to the teacher of a technical kind; that is, programmes may be relayed to the children at the behest of the teacher, and some are directly produced—as schools broadcasting —for this purpose. It adds considerably to the resource of the teacher, joining with tape-recorders, film-projectors and much other gadgetry of an electronic brand. At its most radical, as deployed by the Open University, it has prompted the concept of 'distance' teaching, now being pioneered in developing countries by agencies like the International Extension College. Whilst yet on a small scale and directed only at a tiny group of mature students, it has added a vivid fillip to the design of old-style correspondence courses, for it conceives, by implication, of the home-bound student. In historical terms the school, as the educational locus for what the Victorians called 'the popular orders', is of late and short-term duration. Normally, throughout history, children have been, save for the élite, schooled in the bosom of the extended family, and it is a wry conceit to visualize, via television and allied electronic aids, a brisk retreat back to the home for the educand.

In turn, this raises harrowing questions of employment. Arguably, the cleverly and colourfully produced television presentation might prove more efficient than what some might regard as the vapid ramblings of hundreds of second rate teachers on site. Add the other miracles of micro-electronics—the computer, the calculator, several forms of recall equipment, all in miniaturized form—and the day of self-automated tuition may soon be nigh. In other words, with £50 at today's prices buying £200,000 worth of 1960 computer wizardry, those slivers of silicon, those microchips which threaten to revolutionize the economy, could also effect not just the approach but the very existence of teachers, just as they put at risk the working life of many other craftsmen. The liberal answer—the need for a face-to-face human liaison—will be elegantly pressed, and, over the coming years teachers must perforce come to terms with technology. Of the controversial case of the accused poisoner Florence Maybrick, Lord Birkenhead put the question: 'Was she tender nurse or calculating assassin?' Teachers musk ask the same question of technical aids.

In the second place, it is illuminating that teachers, by and large, have seen television as a mechanical support, proffering a modicum of specially made educational programmes. Many have failed to see it as an art-form or, failing that, a social force in its own right. For better or for worse, it is unlikely that children have ever enjoyed or suffered so substantial and coherent a common culture as that dictated by television. It has a thousand all-pervading reference points, and the commercial jingle, spinning from every child's lips, is the folk-lore of the current playground. The Opies of the future will be explaining that this piece of parodied doggerel relates to a building society or soap powder advertisement of 40 years ago, rather as now we learn that 'Ring-a-ring-a-roses' was about the bubonic plague or Jack Horner was a pluralistic ecclesiastical.

That this huge corpus of common culture is not more absorbed into the substance and methods of teaching is evidence, in some minds, that school-teachers are at once backward-looking and arbitrary in their assessments of the curriculum. Although television might be regarded as the nearest to a national art form, it is sometimes ignored, even with contempt, by teachers. They seemingly prefer material beatified by age and wisdom; material which is deemed to have stood the tests of both time and critical appreciation. One has recently gained the impression that cinema, which used vis-à-vis theatre, to be regarded with scorn, has now gained grudging admittance to the curricular pantheon with television the scorned outsider. This raises a basic question about curriculum planning: to what degree should schools adjust to the everday cultural experience of their charges?

Such a supposed adjustment would affect both method and content. It would, in part, be about using the concrete experience of the child to make his exercise in a number of skills more realistic, but it might also be about educating him to become a more critical television viewer. By analogy schools have, not without success, tried to educate people to read, and to read critically and compassionately. Faced with an overtly audio-visual culture teachers might feel obliged to direct their attentions to that objective, and not, as some would rather feebly appeal, leave it to the indirect consequence of other forms of training such as in literature or art. To summarize the case, are we to look forward (and some examining boards, especially in CSE, are not far removed from this) to the 'O' level Television subject, with 'Playschool', 'Starsky and Hutch' and 'Fawlty Towers' as the 'set' programmes?

In the third place, teachers must consider and even pronounce on the interlock of television with social behaviour, in or out of school. The conundrum is simple to spell out: does television encourage violence by example or sublimate its innate tendencies by or through vicarious or proxy channels? The answer is complicated and hotly contested, and one could substitute vandalism, hooliganism, sexual promiscuity and several other purported social ills for violence in that riddle. Researchers clash on this issue. Once more the student should be aware that, as with comics and radio in the previous generation, the verbal toing and froing about the good or evil wrought by cultural innovations is as inexhaustible as it is inconclusive. The student might recall St Augustine's calumny against the theatre — 'those cages of uncleanness and public schools of debauchery' — or hear the puritan sigh 'will not a vulgar play, with the blast of a trumpet, sooner call thither a thousand, then an hour's tolling of a bell to bring to the sermon a hundred?' And the time to refresh the memory with those bitter comments is when trying to cajole a bunch of youngsters to pay a visit to the local theatre to watch a provincial tour of *Measure for Measure*.

What is uncontestable is the remarkable impact of television on the consciousness of children, and the manner in which it shapes their hopes and fears, their taste in music and humour, and their linguistic command. It cannot be ignored. The average viewer watches between two and three hours a day, and for children it is over three hours a day. It bids fair to equal the amount of time spent in active learning in school, and few would dare claim that the school's presentation standards consistently match those of television, however critical they might feel about the content and mores of the programmes.

In the fourth place, television forms part of a broader social ambience. The technology which constructs television sets constructs much else, and the effect on social life is significant. It gradually transforms both working and domestic life by reducing the chores of a more manually-oriented existence. It creates leisure, and, in cyclic response, it creates mechanistic cushions for that leisure. However brilliant its glories, television would not be viable unless millions had the time to watch. Leisure may mean early and, because of improved health facilities, longer retirement; it may mean shorter hours and longer holidays; it may mean stark unemployment. Television stands as token for the technical processes which invent machines to create leisure time and then to to fill it. This goes beyond the question of direct effects on social behaviour. It encompasses the whole question of educational objectives, which, hitherto, have been marked in modern nations, wisely or unwisely, by an emphasis on the work ethic. But if, in the post-industrial era, the balance of work and leisure is to alter, then maybe schools should concentrate on a more positive approach to leisure. Certainly, in the mid-term, as was hinted in the last chapter, this may produce a conflict between the providers and the users of the service. The difficulty is that automation which, since 1945, has been discussed in terms of leisure possibilities has contrived, with other factors, to produce unemployment figures of well over a million, and these, according to the more pessimistic forecasters, are likely to race well over that mark by the late 80s. Given Britain has a million or so at leisure, but they are, so to speak, the wrong million: underemployment and leisure have not, as actualities, been matched, and the school is left on the horns of a dilemma.

A corollary to this is the pressure on the education service to retain its clientele longer. The knotty equation of higher education and higher economics alluded to in chapter four may perhaps have a third option by way of resolution. This is the custodial notion of the school. When the Newcastle Commission on *The State of Popular Education in England* reported in 1861, it spoke gravely of 'the peremptory demands of the labour market'. It continued 'if the wages of the child's labour are necessary either to keep the parents from the poor rates or to relieve the pressure of severe and bitter poverty, it is far better that it should go to work'. The 'peremptory demands of the labour market', however, have changed in emphasis. By the 1860s, as the Newcastle Commission acknowledged, there were thousands of children with neither work-places nor schools to attend, particularly in the large industrial cities. It is not to wax too cynical to recognize for example, that the prohibition of women and children from working down mines, enforced a quarter-of-a-century earlier, was made possible by improvements in haulage techniques which made them redundant.

So has it continued. It is not difficult to parallel the advance of technology and its consequent effect on the labour-mart with the raising of the school leaving age and the expansion of further and higher education. For a decade or so after the Second World War, national service, by removing almost all 18-year-olds from active industrial service for a 1½ to two-year term, perhaps acted as blotting-paper for superfluous labour. Certainly the raising of the school leaving age to 16 in 1972 had something of this custodial quality. The difficulties of employment for the 16 to 19 age group in the late 70s was met with all manner of government-funded training programmes, under the auspices of the Manpower Services Commission, and some maintenance allowances to those staying at school beyond the statutory mark. It may have been necessary for the good of the economy; what is probably more certain is that it was deemed a political necessity to provide a social corral, however comfortable and inspiring, for children and then youths for a longer period because of the problems of structural under-employment. In one sense, this is the logical outcome of the factory-based economics; once workers were no longer engaged at home and to the extent their children were not needed to assist them in their varied crafts, be it spinning or farming, then the school as a kind of juvenile penitentiary was on the cards. Ironically, and as further evidence of the tangled webs of leisure and employment, the desire or need for women to find jobs has recently created pressure at the other end of the system; to wit, the under fives. Campaigns for extended nursery or day-care reflect some of this same relation between the world of work and the world of children.

Now television has been utilized to illustrate how cultural and social changes may raise queries within the ambit of education and about the school's relation to its community. Several aspects of modern life are of this order. They are not necessarily novel; it may be an accentuation of emphasis which constitutes the change. The pop culture, advertising, the foreign holiday, consumer durables: these spring to mind as but four examples out of many. Each must be examined as one of several parts, the sum of which do equal the totality of the child's social environment. Each may have particular traits, but, in the beginning, each may be analyzed apropos teaching from the four corners of: the technical character of the component under review; its likely involvement with curriculum development; its relation to social attitudes and behaviour; and its place in the social context at large.

What must be emphasized is the fact that teaching is not finally possible in vacuo, and that the whirling kalaidescope of cultural patterns, however meretricious or disturbing to the teacher, will not be thwarted by passive denial.

Essay subjects and seminar topics

1 'Just on this single day, that nightmare is costing the world untold congestion, noise and pollution, some two hundred deaths, many thousand shattered bodies, and between one hundred and two hundred million pounds. Isn't it time we woke up?'

Alistair Aird The Automative Nightmare (1972)

Have teachers awakened to the impact of the motor car, good and bad, on education?

2 '...the *Olympics* (BBC I recurring) settled down to the task of boring you rigid with the track and field events'

Clive James The Observer (1976)

Outline a possible curriculum programme for training juvenile television critics.

6 WHY SCHOOLS?

Narration (with the teacher as narrator) leads the students to memorize mechanically the narrated content. Worse still, it turns them into 'containers', into receptacles to be filled by the teacher. The more completely he fills the receptacles, the better a teacher he is. The more meekly the receptacles permit themselves to be filled, the better students they are.

Education thus becomes an act of depositing, in which the students are the depositories and the teacher is the depositor. Instead of communicating, the teacher issues communiques and 'makes deposits' which the students patiently receive, memorize, and repeat. This is the 'banking' concept of education, in which the scope of action allowed to the students extends only as far as receiving, filing, and storing the deposits. They do, it is true, have the opportunity to become collectors or cataloguers of the things they store. But in the last analysis, it is men themselves who are filed away through the lack of creativity, transformation, and knowledge in this (at best) misguided system. For apart from enquiry, apart from the praxis, men cannot be truly human. Knowledge emerges only through invention and re-invention, through the restless, impatient, continuing, hopeful inquiry men pursue in the world, with the world, and with each other.

In the banking concept of education, knowledge is a gift bestowed by those who consider themselves knowledgeable upon those whom they consider to know nothing. Projecting an absolute ignorance onto others, a characteristic of the ideology of oppression, negates education and knowledge as processes of inquiry. The teacher presents himself to his students as their necessary opposite; by considering their ignorance absolute, he justifies his own existence. The Students, alienated like the slave in the Hegelian dialectic, accept their ignorance as justifying the teacher's existence—but, unlike the slave, they never discover that they educate the teacher.

The raison d'être *of libertarian education, on the other hand, lies in its drive towards reconciliation. Education must begin with the solution of a teacher-student contradiction, by reconciling the poles of the contradiction so that both are simultaneously teachers and students.*

Paulo Freire *Pedagogy of the Oppressed* (1970)

The threat or promise of technical change *vis-à-vis* school structure (touched on in the previous chapter) is but an aspect of the profounder consideration of the school as an institution. It must be recognized that the school, as a training centre for juvenile conscripts, is a novel institution. Although now organized on a worldwide basis, it is a product of the industrial age, and, before that, other forms of induction of the young into adult society were the norm. These were usually based on the home or on some type of apprenticeship, and, where schools as institutions did exist, they were normally élitist. It is a reasonable hypothesis that the governing class or élite will control each society, attempting to use education as an agent of perpetuation and providing its own membership with a privileged brand of instruction. It is often pointed out that the USSR, where education is, in their own phrase, 'directed towards the strengthening of the socialist state', has its Schools of Political Literacy and various kinds of 'Party' schools. Before the 1917 Revolution education was rather more developed in Russia than is popularly thought (there were 6,000,000 children in state schools just prior to the Revolution) but this included the so-called Classical Schools for the nobility.

This illustration is valuable because it demonstrates that this governing class syndrome operates whatever the political apparatus and ideology. An obvious parallel with the Russian Classical Schools are the English Public Schools which stamped the youth of our own ruling classes in the required mould, and, to some degree, still do—80% of Britain's leading judges and the directors of its major banks and insurance companies are ex-public schoolboys.

By extension, it might be anticipated that the deployment of schools for all classes would not necessarily change that motivation, and the Victorian debate about popular education reflects this. For a mixture of religious, political, vocational and civic reasons, the Victorians reversed the older view that literacy permitted access to seditious material and was thus to be thwarted by, for instance, severe taxation on paper and on the press. By 1847 Macaulay was able to preach that 'the education of the common people is the most effectual means of protecting persons and property'.

It is this suspicion that the school is a control mechanism for and on behalf of those holding power which is at the base of the current critique of schools as institution. It is this characteristic which Ivan Illich, who, along with Everett Reimer, is the school's most incisive critic, calls 'manipulative'. It stands, along with law enforcement agencies, mental hospitals and other devices, at one end of the 'institutional spectrum', with others—telephonic, postal and other communications, parks, shops, and so on—at the opposite or 'convivial' end. These are 'institutions men use', according to Illich, 'without having to be institutionally convinced that it is to their advantage to do so'. He and his followers would wish to see education transformed from the 'manipulative' to the 'convivial'. Illich writes in his celebrated *De-Schooling Society*:

Schools are designed on the assumption that there is a secret to everything in life; that the quality of life depends on knowing that secret; that secrets can be known only in orderly successions; and that only teachers can properly reveal these secrets...New educational institutions would break apart this pyramid. Their purpose must be to facilitate access for the learner: to allow him to look into the windows of the control room or the parliament, if he cannot get in by the door.

In the place of schools Illich would develop 'learning webs', patterns of learning exchanges available to all. Even his sympathisers wonder whether these 'skills exchanges' might not be too sophisticated for that openness of access so passionately desired by Illich, but there now exist, through such means as televisual retrieval of information by telephonic control, elaborate examples of his proposition.

This pessimistic view of the school is a newer response. The radical element in Western politics has long espoused education as the chief instrument in the struggle for reform—'the first thing we need is education' said Robert Blatchford, the pioneer British socialist and author, in 1894, of *Merrie England*, and the echo of that sentiment rings down the years. It produces an odd four-handed contest: conservatives worried lest overmuch schooling make for too much mischief; conservatives anxious to school for the preservation of the status quo; radicals keen to school for the creation of mischief; radicals doleful that schooling is manipulative and fundamentally illiberal.

What the argument really concerns is the control of knowledge and information, and there is some confusion between education, as a corpus of such materials, and education, as a channel of or governor on such information. There are those, usually now categorized under the heading of 'alternative education', who accept the generality of the Illichian analysis but eschew its extremism. They argue that different rather than no schools could be the answer, schools dissociated from the state or the church or any other kind of predisposition or vested interest. The progressive movement in primary education especially stemmed partially from this view, usually founded in a belief that education was about self-realization rather than 'mechanical obedience'. It is traceable to the beginning of this century and, sporting names like Froebel, Montessori and Dewey, could proudly claim to be international.

The effects of such thinking on British infant schools (frequently used by American radicals as examples of the de-schooling art) is well-known, while a number of independent schools, eager to press beyond the bounds of what the state system would countenance, also flourished. The most notable of these is probably Summerhill, opened in 1921 by A. S. Neill with the objective, derived from Freudian psychology, of liberating education from authoritarian tenets and allowing the emotions precedence over the intellect. This mantle has been inherited by the 'free school' movement in Britain, with the White Lion Free School in Islington as perhaps the longest runner. These schools remain independent of the maintained system, but are not (like Summerhill and *avant garde* boarding schools like Bedales) fee paying; indeed most Free Schools deliberately choose socially disadvantaged areas on the ground that the alienation from the state system of children there is most pronounced.

Thus to adapt Ivan Illich's 'institutional spectrum', we find, in Great Britain, a gamut of schools from the traditional and heavily-disciplined and didactic to the progressive and libertarian and self-regulated. As with the political spectrum, it manages, in some senses, to gyrate into the circular, for both extremes proclaim that self-reliance is their main objective. What is intriguing is that the extremes are both independent. Private schools represent the nearest approaches to deschooling as, in the draconian regimes of some boarding schools, they most potently exhibit the harshest instances of autocratic schooling. In between, and catering, it should not be forgotten, for 95% of the children, are the state schools. A general impression is that, nowadays primary schools lean towards the former, and secondary schools, beset with examination worries, toward the latter.

All have teachers, and all but the most esoteric models have some teaching manifestation, even if it is only the active parent or what Illich calls the 'skill teacher'. It is the role in which the teacher casts him or herself which is critical. To employ an old-fashioned term, the 'institutional spectrum' has a notation of strictness in its professionals. There are teachers who insist on a dogmatic and formal approach, regarding the child's mind, after John Locke's phrase, as a 'blank sheet', and the teacher's task to transmit knowledge to the coming generation. This age-old view of the tutelary role is now challenged by the more open-ended definition of the teacher as facilitator, as the lubricant of the student's drive toward self-realization. The rather attractive tone of the fresher definition should not dissuade the teacher-in-training from an earnest appraisal of its implications. For instance, the anti-Illichian might suggest that, without certain skills, the child is not capable of exercising these kinds of choices about knowledge and that it is therefore in the child's best interest to formalize his instruction somewhat.

Conversely, the suspicion that the teacher is the tool and servant of an oppressive state machine, ensuring the obedience of the masses, is no melodramatic emotion. It draws attention to the Shavian dictum that 'all professions are conspiracies against the laity'. It is not only in education, but in medicine, the law, officialdom generally, and indeed among all groupings of experts, like architects and media specialists, that the accusation might be levelled. Much of our civic life concerns a series of professional-lay dialogues, and teachers can most vividly appreciate the problem when, as lay-persons, they find themselves locked in mortal combat with their doctor, their solicitor, their bank manager, their inland revenue inspector, their city surveyor, and so forth. From behind the defences of prescribed qualifications and unintelligible argots, professionals frequently obtain and sustain power over their particular clientele. There is little doubt, for example, that should a clear case be made out in England for a mammoth de- or reschooling process which would require very few specialists, that case would founder on the powerful and indomitable force of organized labour, that is, the teaching organizations. Rightly, their first task needs must be the protection of their memberships, and, like all other crafts and professions, the instinct for survival is stronger.

Much of this indicates that the consideration of the nature of the school as institution is but a facet of an overall analysis of society. A society and its education system are joined in a cyclic process, each helping to determine the other. Radicals are eager to alter schools that society might be that much nearer alteration; they are as enthusiastic to alter society, in the knowledge that schools would then perforce be altered. The Illichian title — *Deschooling Society* — is very apt: he uses the school as a metaphor for the 'manipulative society'. Others, more optimistic, would claim that our society is not as oppressed and 'mis-educated', to use Reimer's word, as the gloomier critics believe, that its pluralistic, democratic and open-ended tendencies are genuine and firm, and that its schools should, must and are already following suit. This more revisionist stance would take heart from the informality of method and of mores in some schools and the attempts there to offer opportunity for wide ranging heart-searchings about the issues facing children. One's impression is that, if faced with the question at its purest, many teachers now would, in describing their position, opt somewhat uneasily for a compound of giving strong leads and persuasive openings to their charges. Perhaps that piece of uncomfortable fence-sitting is not inappropriate today. British society itself appears to accept a muddled compromise of wanting its citizens both to be mutely obedient and to think stoutly for themselves. If this be the rule, then teachers must remember that, after teaching children to stand on their own feet, they shouldn't be surprised if sometimes the children step on the teachers' toes.

This situation relates once more, then, to the mainsprings of social life and action. The compromise in effect, is that between the state, with part-control, and the individual, with part-freedom. John Stuart Mill spoke of a civic equation in which there was discipline in all that concerned the community and liberty in all that concerned the individual. This is an excellent rule of thumb, except that, in practice, the borderline between community and individual is none too precise. Nowhere is this better exemplified than in the schools, for we have a pronounced division between private and public education. The private or independent schools, although affecting very few children directly, have a compelling psychological effect, and it is as well to recall that the public system, large as it is, is an accretion to rather than a replacement of the older, private component.

In this it is matched by its fellow public sector agencies, for the collectivist trend in the United Kingdom has ever been about additions and not substitutions. The National Health Service leaves a significant residuum of private medicine, including the curious ambivalence of its own contractual arrangements with doctors and other professionals. Council houses, although they have increased considerably, are still outnumbered two to one by owner-occupied or privately-rented houses, while the social services have not completely replaced private pensions, old-people's hostels and so on. Even the law, with its chief professionals, the lawyers, very much in the private segment, and with private security forces on the increase, is not free from this dichotomy.

For citizens and particularly teachers this poses a philosophic conundrum: Is education a matter for the community or the individual, or, if both, for which in larger measure? Should those willing and able to pay for what is regarded by some as a superior schooling be regarded with approbation, for acting so selflessly on behalf of his children, or with disapproval, for thereby penalizing other children (perhaps in greater need) in the quest for education? One way of looking at the question is to ponder whether education is a principle, like justice, which, for the betterment of the community, should be negotiated and distributed in even-handed style, or a commodity, like a washing-machine or a holiday, which, for the benefit of the individual, should be left to personal choice and wherewithal. An added point for teachers is to wonder whether, having been trained at public expense in university or college, it is completely ethical to obtain employment in a non-maintained school. Incidentally, the issue applies at both ends of the 'institutional spectrum', for those, as teachers or parents, who opt out of the public and into the independent schools, however progressive and non-profit-making, are open to something like the same inquiry.

A major technical problem is that, despite the wide range of schools, there are, legally, only the two alternatives. Like the biblical division between the quick and the dead, there are no shades of distinction: there are only public (i.e. state) and private schools. In practice, this underlines the institutional issue, for the great majority of children attend what, ultimately, are centrally-controlled schools, with a tiny minority paying to attend what are almost all schools of a traditional cast. One suggestion is that a third option be allowed of the devolved or co-operative school, with a group of like-minded teachers and parents operating the school autonomously and on an entirely decentralized basis, but funded from the public coffers so that lack of private means would be no hindrance. This issue is also relevant to population shifts (see chapter 9) and accountability (see chapter 15).

But crucial to this whole institutional survey are professional attitudes. Knowledge of itself is passive, to be made alive, according to their lights, by such as teachers. It has been wisely said that God sends meat and the devil sends cooks.

Essay subjects and seminar topics

1 'A general state education is a mere contrivance for moulding people to be exactly like one another'.
   This was said by a man who believed 'free government required the public education of the citizens'. Can one reconcile this seeming contradiction in the operation of the average school?

   J. S. Mill On Liberty (1859)

2 Many teachers say they just want to be left to get on with the job of helping children learn and that abstract debates about for instance, 'the institutional spectrum' are irrelevant. Have such teachers buried their heads (i.e. ostrich-like, not homicidally!) in the sand to the point where they constitute a menace to the children's political and social well-being?

THE SOCIAL STRUCTURE OF EDUCATION

7 THE SCHOOL POPULATION

I doubt whether it would be desirable, with a view to the real interest of the peasant boy, to keep him at school till he was 14 or 15 years of age. But it is not possible. We must make up our minds to see the last of him, as far as the day school is concerned, at 10 or 11. We must frame our system of education upon this hypothesis; and I venture to maintain that it is quite possible to teach a child soundly and thoroughly, in a way that he shall not forget it, all that is necessary in the shape of intellectual attainment, by the time that he is 10 years old.

Rev. James Frazer, later Bishop of Manchester,
in his evidence to the Newcastle Commission, set up in 1858

This report is about the education of English boys and girls aged from 15 to 18...If we are to build a higher standard of living — and, what is more important, if we are to have higher standards in life — we shall need a firmer education base than we have today...

There are two main arguments for raising the school-leaving age. One starts from the social and personal needs of 15-year-olds, and regards education as one of the basic rights of the citizen; the other is concerned with education as a vital part of the nation's capital investment...A boy or girl of 15 is not sufficiently mature to be exposed to the pressures of the world of industry or commerce.

The Crowther Report (1959)

Almost exactly a hundred years separated the Newcastle Report from the Crowther report. Both adopted a similar ideology in the best interests of the child—and both agreed that a modicum of education was a prerequisite for a realization of this kindly objective. But each had a diametrically opposed view of what this meant in time spent in schooling; indeed, the implied optimum in Crowther and its successors of schooling until 18 involved in a doubling—13 or 14 years from four to six years—of the mean advised by many commentators a century before.

Because of this fundamental change of approach, the school population has expanded on two fronts—lengthier durations of schooling, and population increases at large. It was also suggested in an earlier chapter (chapter 2) that the demographic explosion was one cause of extended schooling.

Initially, it might be useful to erect a simple statistical frame of reference, including a projection of future prospects. These approximate figures are for England and Wales, and the school population figures are public sector only, and all figures have been brusquely rounded up for ease of understanding.

Date	Population in millions	School population in millions	Ratio
c.1870	22	1.5	1:15
c.1900	32	5.5	1:6
c.1950	43	6.0	1:7
c.1970	49	8.0	1:6
c.1980	49	8.5	1:5
c.1985	50	7.5	1:7

The graph drawn from these percentages would not be a regular one. At the time of the first major education act in 1870 about 1,500,000 children were in receipt of government-funded schooling 'more or less imperfectly', as Forster wryly put it. His own view was that as many again between six and 12 (and one might hazard the estimate of some 200,000 under six) were 'not on the registers of government schools'. Had they been, the ratio would have been close to 1:7, not far from the 1900 figure. In fact the 1900 figure represents a nation, not much different in population structure from 1870, but now with a free and compulstory system from five to, with exemptions, 13.

The somewhat startling figure of nearly 6,000,000 (13.5% of the population) in 1950, is not, of course, caused by some gratuitous piece of administrative reaction. It reflects two features: one is the increasing average longevity of life as health and nutrition improved over the century; and the other is the plateau in terms of birth rate which had begun in the years after the First World War and had been sustained steadily during the Second World War. There were several causes for this: the absence on active service and the savage loss of life among young men, especially in the First World War; the reluctance in such parlous time to start families; a move toward smaller families, with improved birth control in practical support of such sentiments. Interestingly the highest number of grant-aided pupils prior to the 1950s was about the end of the First World War, when 6,250,000 were on the school rolls. That was in pursuance of the 1918 Act which raised the school leaving age for most children to 14.

From then until after the last war the school population hovered at or just below the 6,000,000 mark. Then came the so-called 'bulge' in the post-war birth rate, as thousands settled hopefully for a peaceful future and, once more, better dietary and medical habits assisted. In 1947 the 1944 Act, raising the leaving age to 15, came into effect and by the end of the 50s, the numbers in school had shot up to 7,000,000.

By now the numbers staying on at school beyond the statutory age as well as those starting earlier in public sector nursery schools, were beginning to tell. Approaching 500,000 were in these categories in 1960. With the raising of the school-leaving age to 16 in 1972, with pressure on more and more pupils to remain in sixth forms and with further advances on the nursery front, these figures reached a new high in the 70s. In 1975 and 1976 the school population reached what well might be an unassailable record: 9,000,000. Of these, 750,000 were under five or over 16. With children in assisted or independent schools included this meant that over 20% of the population were in schools.

This was a dramatic increase, jumping well beyond the percentage of the population in school in the wartime period, and even overtaking the high proportion of the 1920s. It had many repercussions in such fields as school-building and teacher training, as the education service felt pressurized both for space and personnel. Unluckily, it was a short-lived and somewhat illusory phenomenon, for almost as rapidly, the birthrate began to decline. The fall was from an annual average of 830,000 births in the 60s to 620,000 in the late 70s. More efficient family planning, changes in work patterns with women tending to stay at work longer after marriage; these, and other factors, produced a switch in the fertility stakes, and the school population began to fall. In the short run, the decrease is as troublesome as was the increase. The two most affected components then—buildings and teachers—are the two causing most anxiety now, with threats of school closures and teacher unemployment.

It is reckoned that in 1985 the school population will be not much more and probably less than 7,500,000, a drop of a million; and with perhaps a further loss of nearly a million, by the end of the decade. The 'low' projection for 1991 is 6,600,000 with signs of an upturn in the last years of the century. As the decline naturally bites at the primary stage first—and it began about the mid-70s—the loss there will be in the region of 25%, from 5,000,000 to 3,500,000. Later the secondary echelons will suffer the same swingeing cuts following their 1978/79 peak of 4,000,000.

All this means problems for teachers, and particularly young teachers. The teacher-training programme, so extravagantly enlarged in the 60s, was as cavalierly decimated in the 70s (see chapter 9). In an astringent economic period, the natural advantages, of smaller classes in larger spaces is not unduly attractive, and, by and large, the rigidities of the education system—its failure to prove resilient and flexible in the face of demographic and other factors—is all too patently illustrated by the plenty of the 60s no less than the dearth of the 80s.

The proportion of the population in full-time public education, including under-fives, is currently about 19%, or roughly one in five of the population. But to this must be added, for a more complete picture, those in higher and further education. In 1975 there were 4,240,000 students in higher and further education establishments, including evening institutes, which accounted for nearly a half of the total; 480,000 were full-time HE or FE students, of whom 270,000 were at universities.

In summary, it means that there are presently 9,000,000 pupils and students in full-time education in England and Wales, ranging from the nursery to the university stage.

Looking beyond that into the 1990's, the projections are naturally more variable. According to variants in the fertility rate, the school population in mid-90s could be anything between 6,500,000 and well over 8,000,000. What seems certain is that it will not return quite to its peaks of the 70s—unless, of course, another factor—the raising of the leaving or the lowering of the starting age—is contemplated.

What is also certain is that we are witnessing a change in the population structure. The crude ratios of our little opening table above indicate this, with the mid-80s registering a proportion of school children to population of a pre-war brand, that is 1:7, as opposed to the 1:5 of the late 70s. This is happening not just because of a drop in the birth rate but because of the alternative swing of the pendulum: in 1974 the largest element in the population was the five-to-15 age-range, with 9,000,000, but that group is steadily working itself through and into the labour market. Beyond that, we have with an unprecedented proportion of the population who have retired. Earlier retirement contributes to this but, more important, people are living considerably longer. Present day western society is the first ever to be faced with a large fraction of its population who have completed their working life. The figure is now in the order of 10,000,000: 20% of the population. A picturesque instance of this trend is the fact that, in 1951, there were 141 British centenarians: in 1971 there were 2430, with a post office bonanza developing in congratulatory telegrams from the Queen.

If one assumes that the number of women working—roughly 40% of the total—stays constant, then one might project a situation in the mid-80s where, out of a population of 50,000,000, as many as 30,000,000—easily the majority—are not economically employed, being babies, or in full-time education or non-employed females or retired. Count in some of the social implications of a possible run-down in the labour force because of electronic and other advances, be they straightforward unemployment or a preferable planned schedule of shorter working hours, by day, week or year, and it all adds up to an enormous *volte-face* in the traditional pattern. It could mean vastly increased scope for education, for vocational recycling, or, to put it plainly, sheer time-killing, albeit of, one would hope, a positive kind.

The education system has forever been closely aligned with the economic system in terms of the clientele of both. Since the 1830s an uneasy balance between the two can be traced, with the labour market governing the time that could be devoted to schooling in a mix of several ways. These included the needs of the labour mart for actual personnel and the economy's requirement that they should be more or less educated. Increasingly, employers have needed personnel later, in terms of age, but with improved literacy or numeracy, simply because the economy has grown more elaborate. Further, the point mentioned in chapter 5 must be reaffirmed; that teachers act as custodians of children while adults work, a fact that is reinforced by the tendency of females as well as males so to do.

There would seem to be an unholy alliance between educational provision and socio-economic needs. As the economy required a greater proficiency of education in its work-force, so was the education service expanded, an expansion governed by the capacity of the economy to release its labour-force. In the 1850s and 1860s there was a point reached, especially in large towns, where youngsters had neither work to do nor schools to attend. The impetus of this on educational reform was enormous, nor will it be lost on readers that the 1970s reflect a not dissimilar situation, and the sophisticated administrative structure of the modern industrial state requires civic as well as vocational literacy. With increased unemployment resultant upon, it would seem, a mixture of economic difficulties and economic advances, the problem has grown.

The question is whether these radical alterations in population structure and employment patterns (and few surveys estimate less than 1,500,000 unemployed in the 1980s) will create as revolutionary a change in the education service. If those, so to speak, in need of the beneficient custody of the school are becoming fewer in terms of the conventional young and more in terms of the old, the unemployed and the underemployed, then a system of recurrent or lifelong education may, whatever its other philosophic and moral justifications, be forced on the nation under economic duress. That is, the education service may increasingly have to provide recreational and leisure educational facilities for adults at intervals during their lives, as well as the usual induction phase from four or five onwards to adolescence. Educational history in the United Kingdom describes an onward march of education for all through the elementary and into and through the secondary stage, and soon the world of post-school education, the preserve of the minority (just as, in previous stages, secondary and elementary schooling had been in turn the preserve of the minority) may become perforce open to everyone.

This would fit with that allied determinant of educational provision, the factor of social cohesion. Unemployment is high and considered most traumatic among young people. It does seem that since the end of conscription—at the end of the 1950s—unemployment, and with it concommitant social problems, has increased. The further fear of sporadic unemployment throughout the age groups (by 1994, for instance, the peak schoolchildren of the mid-70s will be in their prime in the 25-35 age range) and the unique phenomenon of 20% of the population in retirement could lead to social catastrophies and stresses not yet imaginable.

It has normally been the governmental response, from the time of Lord John Russell, to use the education services as a benign police or moral crusade to combat social stresses, and indeed the 100,000 youngsters who, at any time in the late 70s, were to be found on the various training programmes chiefly organized by the Manpower Services Commission, might have viewed themselves as within an education as much as an economic system. Perhaps, over the career-span of teachers just commencing or preparing for work, successive governments may gradually construct a lifelong rather than an 'apprentice bound' education service, in part to guarantee the sustenance of the social fabric. (See also chapter 27).

Essay subjects and seminar topics

1 According to the Statistical Office of the European Communities (1978) 6,000,000 of the adult (14-65) population of 166,000,000 in the EEC received vocational training in 1975 compared with 50,500,000 in full-time education. A third of the 6,000,000 are aged 18-24, and 25% (Germany 30%, France 25%, the rest 20%) were British. Discuss.

2 Some schools are turning to joint child/adult classes. Weigh the pros and cons of this method and devise a one-year programme for such a mixed class of 30 in a chosen area of study.

8 SOCIAL COMPOSITION

There once was a man who said 'Damn
I suddenly see what I am.
I'm a creature that moves.
In predestinate grooves.
I'm not even a bus; I'm a tram!

The brand of sociological Calvinism implicit in that age-old limerick is at the crux of the argument about the relation of education to social class. Does the school act as a change-agent, redirecting children into different 'grooves' from those of their parents, or is it primarily an agency for affirmation, the stamping of the educational seal on the parcel of life-chances already decided by birth? A prior point is that, irrespective of what it is now, Britain has never been a caste-society, with iron rigidity of birthrights. It has ever been a class society, with mobility, both social and geographical, rather more evident than has sometimes been thought, even in medieval and early modern times. Thomas à Becket and Thomas Wolsey are both examples of upward mobility, with the church as the significant vehicle.

It is also of interest to note that, until recently, the question would not have been put, simply because the ascriptive nature of society included an overt recognition that social class determined educational opportunity. Schools were (or, more often, were not) available as an aspect of God's making of his creatures high or lowly and ordering their estate. An admixture of social status, cultural background and economic well-being dictated that only the privileged minority would attend schools and universities which were basically intended for the scholastic procreation of the upper classes. The public schools, especially in the nineteenth century, were the basic training camps for the governing and commercial classes, in the belief (not, incidentally, shared and assuredly not stated by the commonsensical Duke of Wellington: the coinage is of much later vintage) that the Battle of Waterloo was won on the playing-fields of Eton.

It is as well to recall that the advent of public education was a social service intended for the succour of the popular orders, and W. E. Forster, author of the 1870 Act and son of a well-respected Bradford Quaker-cum-wool family, felt the School Boards should provide educational rudiments for 'masons, carpenters, tailors and simple policemen'. It was, at best, a second-rate schooling for second-class citizens, and not envisaged as anything like on a par with private education. But, as education was increasingly collectivized, the mood and the philosophy changed, to the juncture where, alone among the social services, the greater need is not the yardstick for the larger provision. Whereas the poorer, or sicker, or more criminal one is, the more treatment or attention one receives, in education the process has been reversed. It is a truism which needs firmly to be placed in this perspective that the cleverer one is, the more one receives by way of provision.

By 1944, and over the following score or so years, this gigantic reversal reached its apex when it was widely believed that, by a massive outlay on a free education service, schooling was open to all the talents, irrespective of social background. The optimistic educators of the 1920s and 30s had eagerly anticipated this millenium, for it was felt that education, gratis and culturally unbiassed, would somehow unshackle the bondage of social ascription. It must be urged that this was, neither in theory nor practice, an egalitarian dream. It never proposed that children should be proffered equal dishes from the educational table, leave alone that those most nearly starving might have the more largesse pressed upon them. Aptly satirizied by Michael Young, it celebrated 'the Rise of the Meritocracy', and was the culmination of the Victorian opinion that man should be rewarded according to the diligent application of his God-granted but widely varying abilities.

The Victorian adoration of competition, reflecting the influences of classical free trade and of Darwinian doctrines, led to the examination mania which dated from 1850 and which is unabated today. Stemming first from the need for what Sydney and Beatrice Webb called the 'prescribed qualification' in professions like the army and the civil service, it gradually permeated downward through the age-ranges. Exams provided rungs on that late Victorian concept, 'the oft-mentioned educational ladder', and, for close on a hundred years, doughty pioneers struggled to make that ladder more readily available. By the time of the 1944 Education Act many believed the objective had been achieved and that, through the 11-plus test, the School Certificate or later General Certificate of Education examinations, and adequate student grants, the ladder from the gutter to the university had been erected. Equality of educational opportunity was hailed as a moral and democratic right and as a surety against social waste.

The shattering of this vision on the rock of harsh reality is perhaps the bitterest disappointment suffered by progressive educators this century. Put simply, the many people, of different political and philosophic shades, who felt equal opportunity to be both fair to the individual and efficient for the nation had grossly overestimated the capacity of the school to bring about change. The domestic and environmental background of children so dictates their response to whatever education offered them as to make the school the weaker element than the home and surrounds in determining educational attainment. The ideal of the educational reformers—that latent ability would emerge if judged and treated dispassionately in the schools—has been foiled because education cannot and does not occur in a vacuum.

Something of this had been noted at the very time when standardized intelligence and other tests were coming to the fore for selection purposes. Kenneth Lindsay, in his *Social Progress and Educational Waste* published in 1926, concluded that 'success in winning scholarships varies with almost monotonous regularity according to the quality of they social and economic environment'. But the serious nature of this imbalance was not sufficiently considered until the post-1944 period when, principally under the aegis of the sociologist A. H. Halsey, the debate was forcefully pressed. In 1956 *Social Class and Educational Opportunity* with Halsey, Jean Floud and G. Martin as its authors, demonstrated the manner in which social classes affected children's grammar-school opportunities. In 1964 J. W. B. Douglas, in his *The Home and the School* suggested that at all ages children of the 'same measured ability' perform differently according to their social categories.

The grand reports of the 60s—Crowther, Newsom, Robbins, Plowden—all leaned heavily on this thesis. Before that *Early Leaving*, a Central Advisory Council Report of 1954, pointed out that only half of those unskilled workers' children one might have anticipated finding in grammar schools had in fact entered one, that two-thirds of these left with fewer than three 'O' levels, and that indeed almost a third left before the end of their fifth year. To highlight the problem one might turn to the National Children's Bureau findings on seven-year-olds and reading. The average difference in reading, at age seven, as between children from social class I and social class V homes was 17 months; and the difference if the children's parents had stayed on at school beyond the statutory leaving age was six months; and the difference where children lived in overcrowded and unsatisfactory conditions could be as much as nine months.

An important point lies in the comparisons among children of the same latent ability—Robbins calculated, for example, that the top third of grammar school children, as graded in 1960/61, who eventually obtained five 'O' levels, included 91% of the 'professional and managerial' but only 49% of the 'semi- and unskilled' children in that cohort. The genetic factor perhaps cannot be overlooked, but it seems not to have the formidable influence of the social factor.

It appears, then, that the spoils do not necessarily go to the intellectual victors, but that the 'meritocrats' of today are the 'aristocrats' of yesteryear racing in different colours. The relationship of social class to educational achievement is not, however, a direct nor simple one. What social class labels approximately do is to indicate a mesh of circumstances which, for good or ill, determine how and to what degree children will partake of the education service.

These conditions include type of income, housing and domestic conveniences, local amenities of various kinds, the important aspect of health, the cultural context in which the child lives, the parents' educational and career backgrounds, their hopes, fears and aspirations, and a number of other factors. Together these mould the child's receptivity to all the school offers.

I recently prepared, for a chapter in the National Consumer Council's *Why the Poor Pay More* (1977) a profile of all English and Welsh leas. This sketch attempted to demonstrate the interlock of the social and the educational. It listed the social composition of the area on a non-manual/manual or middle-class/working-class basis, and added an 'educative dimension' by way of the percentage of the population holding university degrees. Against this were set three items relating to provision—the pupil-teacher ratio, the proportion of children in the population, and the average expenditure on each pupil. It is often argued that socially disadvantaged children suffer through lack of resources or, more generally, that a vast investment in schooling necessarily produces improved results. Lastly, the numbers of young people currently engaged in higher education was included as an outcome. A typical 'high', 'low' and 'middle' instance from this table of 104 authorities is reproduced here.

Local education authority	Bromley	Leicestershire	Sandwell
Non-manual % of population	63.1	38.0	23.4
% of population with degrees	13.4	7.9	3.0

Pupil/teacher ratios	21.2	20.1	22.6
% of population on registers	16	19	20
Expenditure per pupil	£295	£265	£275
% of age range at university	14.1	7.0	3.0

One must conclude that with a knowledge of a child's socio-economic status and his parents' cultural-educational quality, one can make a much more accurate prediction about his or her educational attainment than with a knowledge of the sort of education being provided. For a number of reasons, political and otherwise, there is now a fair measure of equality of provision in this country. The children per teacher and the amount of money spent upon them scarcely varies, certainly in relation to the vast difference in outcome in terms of their educational success or otherwise. What we have in England and Wales is uniformity of opportunity: technically, the dreams of the old pioneers have been all too painfully realized.

It is true that, as John Goldthorpe and the Nuffield Social Mobility Group have made clear, social classes alter in compositions over the years due to economic and other changes—the skilled working class, for instance, is somewhat smaller and the conventional middle-class somewhat larger than hitherto. It is also true that—as Professor Michael Rutter's 1979 Report *Fifteen Thousand Hours* demonstrated—individual schools do often influence, for better or worse, their pupil's standards irrespective of outside factors. The Plowden Report (1967) research on home-school relations conducted by Professsor Wiseman suggested—and here one oversimplifies—that apropos educational attainment the home and neighbourhood combined was more influential than the school in the ratio of 82:18, that is, nearly 4:1. Nonetheless, 18 out of 100 points is not to be ignored: it may be a shock for teachers to realize that they are not the be-all and end-all of scholastic achievement, but they should not sniff too much at their marginal opportunity to produce beneficial results.

But although individual children will, as ever, be favoured or penalized according to these chance happenings and although the influence of social background is by no means absolute nor binding, the general tenor of the research of the last 30 years is indicative of its significant impact. The truism must be accepted that equality of educational opportunity without something more nearly approaching equality of socio-economic and cultural conditions is just not possible. The proportion of working class children at university now is not greater than it was in the 1920s, and, although sixth-form places have more than doubled over the last 20 years, their social composition remains obstinately unchanged and predominantly middle class.

This is not a counsel of defeatism for teachers, but it is a recognition that their role must be re-thought. Until recently the popular view was that the school educated, and others—the home, the community—had little effect. What mattered might be the attitude or, it was popularly thought, the ability of the pupil in relation to teacher competence. Now it must be recognized that the equation is reversed, and that the home and the community 'educate', and it is the school which is the weaker partner. There may be arguments about the degree of the social effect, but few would rule it out as other than a potent force.

This raises important professional questions for teachers. Perhaps they should devise different curriculum programmes for different social backgrounds, not to underline this distinction, but to bring, through diversity, more children through to fullfilment. Maybe there should be several roads to the Rome of educational attainment, however defined, and one criticism sometimes levelled at the 'uniform' English school is that its consistent set of values too strongly favours those from the middle-class homes with similar values. Probably more important is the argument which calls for increased parental involvement. If children do well or badly at school according in part to the ability or motivation of the parents to assist their offspring, then possibly teachers would be well-employed in improving the effectiveness of parents in the education process. It is certainly one feature which has not been tried on any large scale, although pioneer experiments in parental participation have seemed promising. More teachers, more books and better buildings, although welcome, appear not to make radical inroads into the imbalance of social class and educational attainment; perhaps an acceptance of the family, rather than the child in vacuo, as the unit for educational treatment, would prove more effective.

This would mean a major change in the cast of teaching, for it would mean teachers operating as adult as well as child mentors, something for which, as yet, their training, traditions and predelictions have not fitted them. My own personal concerns with this theme must be allowed for in judging its import, but my own opinion is that this need to come to terms with the social factor is the most significant challenge facing teachers now. It challenges them to make a fundamental reappraisal of how the educational process takes place and how teachers, given that novel interpretation, might make a rapid and radical adjustment accordingly. Otherwise the educational trams as envisaged in the operating limerick, will never become buses.

Essay subjects and seminar topics

1 'In the railway journey of life, the school is the waiting-room rather than the signal box'. Discuss

2 'The best strategy seems to lie on the side of economic rather than cultural equality, outside rather than inside schools, in social and economic change rather than in educational change.'

R. Boudon *Education, Opportunity and Social Inequality* (1973)

How true is it, as someone said, that reforming schools was like re-arranging the deck-chairs on the Titanic?

9 TODAY'S PROBLEMS

Now for the slice of sausage in to the mouth. Getting your teeth into it. Your teeth. The meaty taste. And the meaty juice, the real stuff. Down it goes, into your belly.

Gone.

The rest, Shukhov decided, for the morning. Before the muster. And he buried his head in the thin, unwashed blanket, deaf now to the crowd of Zeks from the other half as they jostled between the bunk-frames, waiting to be counted.

Shukhov went to sleep fully content. He'd had many strokes of luck that day; they hadn't put him in the cells; they hadn't sent the team to the settlement; he'd pinched a bowl of Kasha at dinner; the team-leader had fixed the rates well; he'd built a wall and enjoyed doing it; he'd smuggled that bit of hacksaw blade through; he'd earned something from Tsezar in the evening; he'd bought that tobacco. And he hadn't fallen ill. He'd got over it.

A day without a dark cloud. Almost a happy day. There were three thousand six hundred and fifty days like that in his stretch. From the first clang of the rail to the last clang of the rail.

The three extra days were also for leap years.

Alexander Solzhenitsyn *One Day in the life of Ivan Denisovich*

The two themes examined in the previous two chapters—the actual numbers in schools and their social composition—combine to create a number of issues with which teachers and educational administrators are currently finding some difficulty. These are internal problems which plainly affect schools day-by-day. This means they affect children day-by-day, determining for each his or her relative packet of educational advantage or the opposite. And, like Shukhov, some will count their blessings. Chief among these problems are falling rolls (already touched upon), urban decay, the multi-racial factor, and the sexist problem.

a Falling rolls

The effect of a declining pupil population is keenly felt by schools in terms of size. The education service is not a flexible one; it is seriously limited by the geographical location of its static delivery-points, the schools, and many of these are now under threat. The present norms are roughly as follows:

	Primary schools	**Secondary schools**
Pupils	300:22%	1000:43%
	200-300:29%	800-1000:20%
	100-200:28%	600-800:20%
	100:21%	400-600:13%
		400:42%

This means, in practice, that about 6% of our primary children are in schools with less than 100 on roll. That's about 300,000 children. They are at hazard because of pressure on local authorities to close schools. It is no new movement, for, in the ten years after the Plowden Report suggestion that 50 to 90 was the minimum viable size for a primary school, some 2200 schools with less than 100 pupils were closed, to say nothing of the many shut down between 1945 and 1967, when the Plowden Report was published. However, with the building of new schools, and the reorganization and enlargement of others, the number of schools in existence stayed fairly constant over the same period at something approaching 23,000 units.

The abrupt decline in the birthrate, coming at a time, in the late 70s, of economic stringency, has meant a wholesale move to close hundreds of schools suddenly. These often are, as has normally been the case, rural schools, but, increasingly, the problem is becoming an urban one, as the falling birth-rate, plus population drift, affects the cores of large cities. For example, the Inner London Education Authority is currently considering the closure of 40 of its 840 primary schools, and that means one in 20. Overall—and according to the ruthlessness with which one inspects the figures—between 4,000 and 7,500 primary schools could be closed over the coming decade. Most of these have falling registers, with little likelihood of short-term increase, and, consequently, most of them employ three or fewer teachers.

The raising of the school-leaving age and the tendency for children to stay on at school has sustained secondary school numbers, but soon the phenomenon will affect the secondary sector. One estimate is that, by the end of the 80s, up to 1,800 of the country's 5,000 or so secondary schools could be closed, as their registers fall below the educational Plimsoll line of 500. Already 500 have fallen below that magic figure. As many as 9000 of our 30,000 or more schools (over a quarter) are thus at risk, and with them the jobs of many teachers. The National Union of Teachers claim that 24,000 teachers are already unemployed.

The arguments for and against closures are fiercely contested, highly detailed and localized, often emotional and as often elaborate. They tend, in summary, to fall into two categories. One is economic, with local authorities arguing that small schools are too extravagant and their opponents pointing out the hidden costs of transporting children to schools a distance away. The other category is educational (although the two frequently become confusingly entwined) with adminstrators pointing out the scholastic handicaps and drawbacks of schools, primary or secondary, unable to offer a wide enough educational scope. Other educationalists see the smaller school as a bonus—closer to home, less stressful and more caring, and, in any event, something obviously desired by the many parents who have embarked on a nationwide compaign against closures. It is, of course, accepted that the vanishing school, rural or urban, is a prelude to the vanishing community, for few young couples are prepared to settle at too far a journey from a school, which, in a broader sense, may or should play its fruitful part in communal life.

Between the extremes of total shutdown and keeping schools open at any cost, one or two other solutions are emerging. One is the practice of 'federation'. Cambridgeshire has primary examples of this device, three or four schools combining under one peripatetic head, and one could visualize a series of secondary schools—this is already done at sixth-form level in some areas—attempting to offer a breadth of subjects with a federate structure. Another solution would be to legislate for a third type of school—one of the legal problems is that schools are, in chief, either state-maintained or private fee-paying establishments. A school controlled by a parent-teacher co-operative could offer a third option. This method calls both sides' bluff. It asks the local education authority to provide the notional per capita cost for each pupil, thus meeting the economic argument head-on, and it asks parents, as a group, to raise any other revenue required, as a sign of their goodwill. An analogy may be drawn with the housing corporation, where public funds and buildings are managed by the tenants co-operatively. These would be 'de-centralized' schools lodged in the custody of given members of the state. (See also chapter 6 on this issue). This is the picture as in 1980. It is, however, a moving picture, with changes occurring almost weekly.

b Urban decay

This issue relates to falling rolls, and, indeed to the third poser under discussion here, the multi-racial facet of the education service. It is about the abandonment of inner-city districts to the old, the poor, the ethnic minorities and, in general, the disadvantaged. Many commentators feel that the decline of population—birth-rates down from 18 per 1000 in 1964 to 11.6 in 1978—is less alarming than the movement of population. The cities seem to be emptying. Greater London lost nearly 500,000—over 6% of its population—between 1971 and 1977, and Merseyside was abandoned by a similar fraction, amounting to close on 100,000 people. This is not unrelated to the massive loss of jobs in heavy industry and its attendant services like transport and the docks. With many of the comparatively large number of jobs in service industries, private and public, located in emerging towns and areas outside the conurbations—and showing, by that token, net gains in population—the chances of a swing back to the cities seems remote.

These inner rings are also characterized by a depressing series of social indices, like appalling housing, unemployment, ill-health, mental and emotional strain, inadequate social and environmental provision, vandalism, high crime rates and, consequently, poor educational results. Hence the talk of our urban crisis, which, in its educational aspect, is a matter now of run-down schools, losing pupils and losing momentum at deplorable rates, and subject often to problems of low staff morale, truancy and indiscipline. Possibly there is nothing wrong in the inner urban secondary school which is not to be found in any secondary school: but there they are wrongs writ large. All the social and economic detritus of the age seems to be piled disturbingly into the middle of the conurbations, and schools, like every other part of that social fabric, suffer accordingly.

The norm for the large city is that its birth-rates have dropped by more than a half over the last 20 years, while the proportion of children moving away before starting school has remained constant at a little over 20%. Couple this with the higher incidence of antiquated buildings (about one in five primary children go to schools built in the last century) in cities, and, to err on the pessimistic side, one could only prophesy that the great conurbations will soon be shells, and unpleasant, even violent, ones at that.

To raise the question is not, of course, to answer it. But teachers must face a period in which the classic syndrome of Goldsmith's deserted village will be visited upon vast tracts of our older, larger towns.

c The Multi-Racial factor

The co-identification of social disadvantage, as rehearsed in the above passages on urban deterioration and the earlier chapter (chapter 8) on social class, with low educational performance is well known. The establishment of Educational, later Social, Priority Areas was the governmental recognition of this, with its extra assistance—'positive discrimination'—for such districts by way of salary increments and other devices. Educationally, the concept of compensatory education embracing various ways of promoting greater efficiency in the learning process of the socially deprived, was developed. There were also steps—the Coventry authority is perhaps the clearest example—to relate schools in such areas more closely with their host communities in order to build a more productive educational springboard for the pupils.

But the imbalance caused by social disadvantage is accentuated by the difficulties to which ethnic minorities seem to be heir. By the 70s 7% of the British labour force were defined as immigrant workers, a fraction similar to other EEC countries, save that a greater proportion in Britain were of Asian or West Indian origin. In 1971 there were over 1,000,000 people in Britain born in the black commonwealth, and there are now another 1,000,000 of the same ethnic origins albeit born in this country. This coloured community, of 2,000,000 has tended to gravitate to the very urban areas which are under considerable stress, and, while not a significant proportion of the general population (about 5% of the adult and 7% of the child population), their proclivity towards concentration is pronounced. Towns like Bradford, Birmingham, Leicester, Wolverhampton and Greater London have 20% and more of their entrants to school from this coloured community. Of the top 12 urban areas with the severest urban blight, nine were among the districts with the highest proportion of immigrants.

As Professor Alan Little has sadly demonstrated, not only are 'immigrant' pupils, with special reference to those of West Indian roots, underfunctioning at a level below the indigenous population at large, they are performing worse than socially disadvantaged white children (see G. Driver 'How West Indians Do Better At School (Especially The Girls)' *New Society* 17 January 1980). Operating thus in a climate by no means attuned to racial harmony, it is not surprising that the West Indian tends to have slightly more behaviour problems and very much greater difficulty in the job market than his indigenous fellow. The cycle of multiple disadvantage wheels on, and, although there have been many gallant endeavours to ameliorate the educational lot of the coloured community, there has been, as yet, no overall and fullblooded national strategy. Great

Britain is no stranger to strangers: its folk are the product of a dozen and more migrant waves.

It is 30-odd years since this latest migration began, and recent legislative controls have more or less ensured that it has ended. It is certainly high time for the devising of a national policy, and it is likely that such a programme would have to be evolved within a remit of dealing generally with the problem of urban deprivation as we approach the twenty-first century.

d The Sexist Problem

Sex discrimination is less overt but may be no less insidious than the racial brand. Rallying to the anti-Chauvinist cause when my five-year-old daughter evinced an interest in nursing as a career, I ventured to suggest she might contemplate doctoring. 'Don't be silly, daddy', she gaily laughed, 'ladies are nurses; men are doctors'. And this despite that fact she had once had a lady doctor. Nevertheless, it is as impossible to purchase a toy male-nurse's outfit as it is a toy female-doctor's kit, and, in the suburban-orientated readers of yesterday and today, Peter helps daddy with the car and Jane helps mummy with the washing-up.

The sexual stereotypes arrive early and are pressed unremittingly, although often it is unconsciously so. It remains to be seen whether the Equal Opportunities Commission, armed with the sex discrimination legislation of the 70s, will make inroads into this problem, which many feel to be intractable, as they search for anything like sexual equality of membership of professions like law, medicine, politics, engineering, architecture and a dozen more. Put simply, girls overall have about half the chance of a university place as against boys, although the proportion staying on in sixth forms is not dissimilar. Even then it is worth recalling that girls from a non-manual background have ten times the opportunity as those from a manual background. Nor is it just in the refined glades of Academe that discrimination exists: in industry, according to the Robbins Report, a third of boys, but only a twelfth of girls, were to be found in day-release classes.

In terms of school organization sexual discrimination operates in two ways. Firstly, there is the retention of the principle of the single-sex school, which many would feel to be against the natural rights of the child. Some research indicates that, other elements being equal, children in co-education do slightly better academically than their single-sex peers, and, in the late 60s, one study suggested that there was a mild correlation between single-sex schooling and early marital breakdown. This seems to indicate that the commonsensical view—that as males and females have for many millions of years survived together there is little point in sundering them for their five secondary years—should be preferred to the suburban stance—that co-education makes overmuch scholastic distraction and physical attraction. Secondly, there are the practical organizational problems in schools, usually illustrated by girls wishing to do metalwork and boys eager for cookery lessons. The sciences seem a special snare in this regard. Teachers—and parents—have some way to go, from the nursery school to the university, to rid the system of its sexual stereotyping. When Professor Brian Simon calculated that the *son* of a Carmarthen solicitor had 180 times the chance of a higher education as the *daughter* of a West Ham docker, he was identifying the dissonance in our education system by region, social class and also by sex.

So the actual numbers in the school population and their social lineage only construct the social framework of schools. Questions of the incidence of that population, urban as well as rural blight, of ethnic, although less now of religious, difficulties, and discrimination by gender fill out that frame. In sum, they amount to the relative social nature of the educational opportunity children enjoy, and the manner in which some are disadvantaged—or over-advantaged—in the choices first schools and then life, in the shape of the employment or housing market, have to offer.

The American educationalist John Dewey, amongst others, has argued that what the benevolent and sagacious parent might hope for his child educationally would be the same as what the sane and rational community would wish for. But one of the justifications of state education has been the need to stand proxy in the absence of consistent benevolence and sagacity amongst parents in order to protect minors and guarantee their rights and opportunities.

The countervailing weighting of liberal doubts and hopes creates, however, some intriguing dilemmas. The Moslem Pakistani school for girls is sometimes defended as a proper response to the aspirations of the parents of that ethnic minority. It is necessary for the social democrat to recall that such a school discriminates among British children on the grounds of race, religion and sex, and would, as far as public funds are concerned, be judged illegal in the United States of America.

Essay subjects and seminar topics

1 Analyze, using practical case-studies where possible, the advantages and disadvantages of closing a small primary or secondary school, employing social and economic as well as educational criteria.

2 Choosing a set of junior readers or other appropriate text-books, attempt to 'bowdlerize' them from the view-point of anti-sex discrimination.

2 EDUCATION AND THE STATE

CENTRAL GOVERNMENT

10 STATE INTERVENTION

There were many legends also in three districts of the Rev. Mr
Bluffer, HMI. He was of the common-room don type: formerly, and
still gourmet: formerly rough to undergraduates; now rough to
managers, teachers, and children; but withall combining a certain
human element and a liberal hand in spending his own money.
'Why,' I once asked, 'did not the managers rise up, and demand
Bluffer's head on a charger?' and the answer was, that old sinner
would at times wash down his advice and criticisms with cheques in
aid of struggling schools.

There was need of some washing. The Secretary of the
Department told me, some time after Bluffer's death, a story of
HMI's behaviour in school. The master was an elderly man of the
village pedagogue type, and his fumbling ways were a little irritating
to an official in a hurry. The first class wanted reading books, and the
old man went off to fetch them; searched in one cupboard
unavailingly; found them in another; collected them; piled them up
in his arms, and limped back.

'LOOK ALIVE MAN!' shouted Bluffer, with a vigorous slap on his
fat thigh. The master jumped: down went the books, and the children
roared.

The manager, who told the story to the Secretary, was a peer of the
realm, and a wealthy one. I think if he had kicked Bluffer out of the
room—say 40s. and costs—and had let the Government grant go
hang, he would have enjoyed himself more on his deathbed—and
thereafter.

But yet, as I said, there was a human element in Bluffer. From
another country school after the inspection the mistress wrote to her
former headmaster:

'Her Majesty's Inspector has been here. He was in a lovely temper.
When he had done, he kissed all the boys, and all the girls: then he
kissed the pupil-teachers; and last, but not least, he did not omit your
humble servant.'

'On ne s'arrête pas dans un si beau chemin', said Mr Pleydell, when
he saluted Julia Mannering after Lucy Bertram. It reminds one also of
the old cottager who learned for the first time that Solomon had had
all those wives: 'Lor, sir, what blessed privileges them early
Christians had.'

Bluffer's last district was in a large town, and a friend of mine was
a manager of a school therein. When the day of inspection arrived,

the rector was away, and my friend being senior curate, was left to receive the great man. He knew Bluffer by reputation, and with commendable prudence enquired at the Inspector's London Club what, as Mr Weller would put it, 'was his partickler wanity'. It was oysters, and oysters accordingly were laid on. On the appointed day the curate approached the official, explained his position as viceregent, and proffered hospitality. The inspector hesitated: to lunch with a curate was hazardous, and, indeed pessimi exempli: but this curate was a Fellow of his college, and had 'sat on good men's feasts, and from his eyelid wiped a tear' when the cook fell short of excellence; it was a long way to the hotel: on the whole he though he would venture.

'And when he came to my lodgings,' the curate reported, 'and saw the oysters laid out on the table, and the brown bread and butter, his face lit up with a heavenly smile and the report was excellent.'

E. M. Sneyd-Kynnersley, HMI. *Passages in the Life of an Inspector of Schools,* (1913)

Although the Tudors had tried to control education and although the Society for the Promotion of Christian Knowledge controlled, by 1729, nearly 1500 Charity Schools on a national basis, the story of state intervention is no more than 150 years old. The SPCK's precedent of nationally based authority, with some measure of local management boards and of inspection, was to have some slight influence on later state action, but its immediate effect was to help ensure that the churches were in the foreground of educational management. By 1818 England's 18,000 and more schools were church-run, principally by the nonconformist British and Foreign Society and the Anglican National Society, itself a child of the SPCK. The religious-secular contest was to be ever present in educational history. The voluntary school was the automatic response of a society denied a political solution to its educational poser: the voluntary school filled the vacuum left by the inaction of the state. Other countries—the USA is a prime example—have largely escaped the dread trap of church-state controversy, but not ourselves, and it is a controversy which is played out in the compulsory assemblies and period of religious instruction in every maintained school to this day.

The state's first act was the celebrated grant of £20,000 in 1833, but other state interference made an indirect contribution. The reform of the poor law and the promotion of the harsh workhouse regime included pauper or industrial schools: by 1854, 30,000 children were being thus educated. The Factory Acts of, for instance, 1833 and 1844 decreed that factory hands between the ages of nine and 14 should have a certain amount of schooling. Neither the pauper schools nor the factory schools were necessarily beneficial.

The first Factory Inspector, Leonard Horner, found one of the latter taking place in a coal hole. In practice, it was this device of inspection which was to be most influential. Following on from factory legislation, the Victorian reforms of the police, the prisons, public health, the poor law, lunacy and other social agencies threw up the corollary of the inspector, sifting around on an itinerant basis to evaluate whether the law was being obeyed—and with typical utilitarian rectitude—whether the state was getting its money's worth. As typical of the rationalizing cost-accountancy of the Utilitarian was the thirst for 'vital statistics', a thirst assuaged by men like William Farr, who coined the phrase. Vast agglomerations of statistics were assembled, centring on the Registration of Births, Deaths and Marriages (implemented from 1839), without which it is impossible to be administratively sure, for example, whether all children of five have started school.

A Committee of the Privy Council on Education was established to superintend this system of grants and inspection, and this Committee was the precursor of today's Department of Education and Science. And those who feel that being Secretary of State for Education is not a prestigious post should take solace from the knowledge that the Vice President of this Education Committee was responsible for rinderpest in imported livestock as well as HMIs. In 1856 he also took under his wing the Department of Science and Arts, which was supposed to encourage further education in those fields. And the overall title changed to Education Department.

That political phase known as the Confusion of the Parties was to ensue until, by the late 60s, the modern Conservative and Liberal parties emerged, and educational policy was no less chaotic than any other during this period. Many factions argued their cases for a pattern of education. There were those who wished to keep the state emancipated from education on the grounds that education and religion were indissoluble and that state action degraded both. There were those—the Secularists, such as Richard Cobden—who would have preferred the adoption from the USA of the Massachusetts System, a local rather than a national system of control. Incidentally, as early as 1827 the Liverpool Liberals, led by William Rathbone, had opened the country's first ever municipal schools, North Corporation and South Corporation schools, but their plan to establish 14 of these interdenominational enterprises was foiled by an alliance of the Conservatives and the Church of England.

That curio, in fact, demonstrates something of the then dilemma. Voluntary schools could no longer support themselves to the degree and in the places necessary to produce full results, but people objected to paying rates or taxes for the sustenance of private bodies of a religious flavour at variance with their own. The Newcastle

Commission (1858/61) concluded that a state-aided voluntary system was the correct approach, but that its efficiency should be improved beyond their since disputed figure of but a quarter receiving adequate instruction. In 1862 the head of the Education Department, Robert Lowe, introduced the rigours of the Revised Code and propounded the doctrine of Payment by Results. In order to keep a careful check on the attendance and performance of scholars at grant-aided schools, he legislated that, instead of grants being paid as an equivalent of amounts raised by voluntary endeavour, they should be based on attendance and examination. 'Hitherto we have been living', said Lowe, that doughty disciple of Adam Smith, 'under a system of bounties and protection. Now we propose to have a little free trade'. He attempted to incorporate a free market with the available grant and certainly succeeded, for one of the only times in administrative history, of lowering the education budget while boosting, in four years, the average attendence from 880,000 to over 1,000,000. 'If it is not cheap', proclaimed Lowe, 'it shall be efficient. If it is not efficient, it shall be cheap.' Lowe did at least tear the flimsy curtain of humanitarian platitudes from round the stark truth of educational politics. In revised form payment by results lasted until 1897 and, some might add, remains today under the less astringent tag of value for money.

It was Robert Lowe again who saw the connection not only between economic dictates but between social inevitabilities and education. Speaking about the 1867-extension of the franchise for working men in the towns, he said 'it will be absolutely necessary to compel our future masters to learn their letters'. The task was left to Gladstone's first cabinet, when, in 1867, his government was returned with 100 majority and proceeded to pass the 1870 Education Act. This was a 'hard compromise', with W. E. Forster forced to steer between the sectarians, hopeful of increased state aid for church schools, and the non-sectarians, ambitious for popularly elected boards to run schools on a nationwide basis. The 1870 Act attempted in Forster's words, to 'fill up the gaps' offering six months grace for the churches to augment their provision (which they did to the tune of 30%, with 4,000 building applications against a normal year's average of 150), before a nationwide survey to ascertain where, failing local initiative, School Boards might compulsorily be formed. These were popularly elected committees on which women could serve, and the Boards could levy a rate and enforce attendance until 13. The debates were bitter; indeed it is likely that Forster, leaving both sides of his party dissatisfied by his balancing act, hereby lost his chance of succeeding Gladstone as the Liberal leader.

Nonetheless, there were soon 300 School Boards and, by 1874, there were 5,000 more schools, making a total of 13,000. Sandon's Act of 1876 legislated for the election of School Attendance Committees in non-board areas, and in 1880 Mundella's Act made, for the first time, education completely compulsory for all children from five to 13, with exceptions on proficiency after ten. In an attempt to stop the voluntary schools from being swamped by the Board schools, a per capita grant of ten shillings was awarded the former, and the indirect effect of this was to end fee-paying in such schools. Elementary school fees were formally abolished in the 1918 Act, and secondary fees in the 1944 Act.

Payment by results and analysis of School Board areas added greatly to the inspectoral role, and determined, despite modern pleas from HMIs that they are in the humane business of 'cross-pollination', the suspicious attitude teachers bear them. At one school of my acquaintance and during a general inspection there, one teacher, washing his hands in the cloakroom, called to, he fondly imagined, a colleague busy behind a closed cubicle door, 'have the bastards been in to see you yet?' 'I am one of the bastards', was the urbane reply, and that may well serve as a summary, except to add that, as originally envisaged, the school, like the factory, inspectors, watched over *private* ventures on behalf of the state. Now they are irrevocably part of the system, and this raises the question of whether an independent inspection service, accountable and open to the public, might not be an improvement.

Another parallel to be drawn with other public services is of the unholy alliance between the central sponsoring and invigilating department and the locally elective board; the General Board of Health and the local Boards of Health, and the Poor Law Commission and the local Boards of Guardians are other examples. This messy bipartite nature of English administration is by no means automatic. Other countries have much more, or much less, centralized systems. Although in Balfour's 1902 Act the Conservatives swept away the School Boards and replaced them with the Local Education Authorities (leas), the Whitehall/Town Hall balance was preserved, as it is in most other public and social services; hence, for example, the spectacle of central government enforcing comprehensive education while sections of local government fight to avoid that destiny.

The overgrown Moby Dick of the School Boards was harpooned by the Conservative whalers, and this arose from the famous Cockerton Judgement. Robert Morant, the somewhat sterile-minded but effective civil servant at the Department, wished to thwart the Boards' 'excessive emphasis' on technical and further education, which they had promoted under cover of the confused definitions of the 1870 Act. Under Morant's guidance, the Secretary of the London County Council Technical Instruction Committee queried expenses at the School Board's School of Art in Camden, and the auditor, T. B. Cockerton charged the Board for them as they were not legally covered by the 1870 Act. Justice Willis ruled against the London School Board, and, immediately and nationwide, hundreds of post-elementary, adult, technical and evening classes were in jeopardy.

There were also fears that the School Boards were, in general, too big for their boots, and that voluntaryism, especially its Anglican branch, was on the wane. Had not the Archbishop of Canterbury said that there was no religious instruction in 316 School Board Areas? As Morant 'the assassin of the boards', argued 'the only way to get up steam...in the face of School Board opposition will be to include in it some scheme for aiding denominational schools'. The 1902 act imposed on the new leas the task of supporting church schools from the rates. There was widespread revolt, particularly among the non-conformists of Wales, and 70,000 were prosecuted for non-payment of rates in the following years. Even on their return to office, the Lords quashed any Liberal attempts to change the position, and the notion that church schools (now called non-provided) should be treated financially almost on a par with the old Board (or provided) schools became entrenched.

In order to obliterate the Boards, the Tories were able to utilize the local government reforms of 1888 which had established a uniform pattern of County Councils and County Boroughs, and these 120 new authorities replaced the 2,500 or more school boards. The new leas had not only a responsibility for elementary schools, be they provided or non-provided (building costs apart), but for taking 'such steps as seem to them desirable...to supply or aid the supply of education other than elementary'. Although political rancour about the liberal dominated boards, the contentious religious question, and preference for conventional rather than technical education thus motivated the authors of the somewhat retrogressive Act, it did at the same time create a uniformity of administration and a spur for secondary education. A co-ordinated national system was introduced after 59 days of acrimonious Commons debate and the application of the closure. The Board had replaced the Department of Education in 1899 (and added the duties of the Science and Art Department) to continue the curious partnership with the leas which had replaced the School Boards. As the prime minister, Balfour, somewhat plaintively said afterwards 'I did not realize it would mean more expense and more bureaucracy.'

That serves as a fitting motto for the state's role in education as the twentieth century opened. It was bureaucracy and finance—to be dealt with in the following chapter—which boomed, while the uneasy partnership of state and local authority continued, with the HMIs attempting, for their part, to take their text from the Book of Daniel: 'many shall run to and fro, and knowledge shall be increased'. The Board of Education became first the Ministry of Education in 1944 and then, in 1964, the Department of Education and Science, and although there have been some revisions in the lea structure, there has been no gainsaying the 1902 proposition that education should locally be controlled as part of a multidisciplinary authority and not, as hitherto, under the auspices of a single purpose agency.

Given that the 1918 Act made not too much of an impact, the first major Education Act after 1902 — and there has been none of such import since — was in 1944. This Act regularized the position of leas, producing a unitary system of some 150 such authorities in England and Wales. The local government reorganization of 1974 trimmed this to 104, in an effort to ensure that leas were rather more of a muchness in size and population. There were, as ever, changes of labels, with the council or provided schools renamed county schools, and the church or non-provided schools divided among aided, controlled and special agreement schools.

The main effect, however, of a rationalized pattern was the sensible decision to abolish the 'elementary' category, which, in many places, had run concurrently with secondary education, chiefly because of the permissive nature of the 1902 Act vis-à-vis secondary schooling. Since 1944 the progressive stages of primary and secondary, with further or tertiary to follow, have been established, with 11 as the normal watershed. Although there has been the introduction of first schools, middle schools and high schools, with varying permutations of age-range, the notion of a systematic progress through a series of stages has been everywhere accepted. Contrary to popular belief the 1944 Act, whilst legislating for universal and free secondary education, did not advocate the tripartite system of grammar, modern and technical schools. These divisions were implicit in the 1926 Hadow Report, the 1938 Spens Report, the 1943 Norwood Report and the 1943 White Paper on Educational Reconstruction: it was the leas who introduced tripartism piecemeal, just, as rather later, they moved in *ad hoc* fashion from selective to comprehensive secondary education, mainly in the 1960s and 70s. Government legislation on comprehension came late in the day, in an endeavour to clean up the few remaining pockets of resistance.

While this demonstrates the virility of the leas, it is also true that, since the war, a change in degree, if not in kind, has taken place, whereby the centralist state has assumed more power. Through fiscal and other controls, like those on teacher-supply and school buildings, for instance, the power of the DES apropos the lea is probably now greater than in the post-1902 period.

It is often said that the 1944 Act was passed in a mood of mellow goodwill because of the fellowship bred by wartime. In retrospect, a likelier explanation is that it was a non-controversial statute (as chapter 22 on secondary education will further testify). It clarified, in politico-administrative terms, the pattern introduced by its 1902 antecedent, but it really did not basically alter the structure of educational governance.

Essay subjects and seminar topics

1 Recalling the terms of the arguments in the 1860s about responsibility for the development of schools, visualize and comment upon
   a the character today of a completely voluntary system with state grants, and
   b the character today of a completely localized system with no state jurisdiction.
2 Evaluate the relative influence on the structure of the state education system of Matthew Arnold, W. E. Forster, Robert Lowe and Robert Morant

11 STATE RESOURCES

Money is like an arm or a leg—use it or lose it

Henry Ford (1931)

For the love of money is the root of all evil

New Testament 1 Timothy vi 10

Get Place and Wealth, if possible with Grace.
It not by any means get Wealth and Place.

Alexander Pope

O, what a world of vile ill-favoured faults
Looks handsome in three hundred pounds a year'

Shakespeare The Merry Wives of Windsor

If you want to know what God thinks of money,
Look at the people he gives it to.

New England saying

'When it is a question of money, everybody is of the same religion.'

Voltaire

The Sheffield Charity School used to sell the nitreous earth from its pupils' dry lavatories to gunpowder manufacturers in order to raise funds, an exercise in what might be called thunderbox economics which is a far cry from today's financial arrangements for education.

Without doubt the most startling and most overwhelming change in public education since the turn of the century lies in the allocation of public funds thereto, an astronomic increase that might be tabled thus:

In the nineteenth century:

1833 £ 20,000: the first ever state grants-in-aid to voluntary societies.

1858 £700,000: as against £24,000,000 on defence — just after the Crimean War.

1861 £813,000: just prior to the Revised Code being introduced.

1865 £636,000: a decline: a tribute to the effect of the 'Payment by Results'.

1872 £1,000,000: not including School Board precepts on the rates: zip! goes the state for £1,000,000 for the first time.

1900 £9,000,000: plus £5,000,000 rates: a total of £14,000,000.

In the twentieth century:

	LEA expenditure	% approx from rates	% approx govt. grant	% local rate on educ.
1910/11	£ 27,500,000	52	48	22
1930/31	£ 82,300,000	47	53	26
1949/50	£ 237,200,000	38	62	33
1976/77	£6,692,000,000	34	66	52

Projected expenditure for 1980/81 was £7,685,000,000, of which some £700,000,000 was for the universities, and the whole an attempt to reduce overall expenditure by 3½%. The £14,000,000 expended annually prior to the 1902 Education Act amounted to 1% of the gross national product. Today's figure is much closer to 10%. Even if that first £1,000,000 figure of 1872 was more realistically, in relation to values a century on, regarded as £10,000,000, it would still represent no more than a thousandth of the current expenditure. In 1968 the DES spoke of the unprecedented growth of public expenditure on education' during the 1960s—the annual increase was 10% throughout that decade; it rose faster than inflation. It is well-known that expenditure flattened out as the heady 60s gave way to the sombre 70s. However, between 1961 (£1,104,000,000) and 1974 (£5,146,000,000) the percentage change was a colossal 366%.

The unease of the central/local see-saw is reflected on the ups and downs of the respective fractions attributable to each. Latterly, the central share has grown, a sure sign that power is tending to flow toward the centre. Yet the percentage of rates expended on education has also grown to over a half, which makes the education service that much more vulnerable to local criticism. The manner in which the tax as opposed to the rate component is calculated is as mysterious as it is mathematical. The current method—but one subject now to critical review—is the Rate Support Grant. In 1977/78, for instance, the proportion of planned local expenditure to be financed by grant was set at 61% as opposed to the previous year's 65.5%. This amounted to (in round figures) £7,000,000,000 of the £12,000,000,000 to be spent, and £1,000,000,000 of this was attributed to specific purposes such as law and order, transport and parks. The remainder—some £6,000,000,000—was the Rate Support Grant, and, in turn, this was divided into three categories: the Domestic Element—£600,000,000 to subsidize ordinary rate-payers; the Resources Element—over £1,700,000,000 to compensate areas whose rateable value falls below the national standard rateable value per head of population; and the Needs Element—£3,700,000,000 to help local authorities maintain particular standards of service. Once this complex formula is solved and each authority receives its award, then, by and large, the RSG is a general grant, about which the authority makes decisions, including the proportion to be spent on education.

The heavy expenditure was very much a characteristic of the 60s. The inter-war years, by contrast, had not been so impressive. The 1918 Education Act sensibly rationalized the bewildering complexities of previous state grants by opting for just two, a block elementary education grant related to pupils, teachers and resources utilized, and a straight 50% higher education grant. But the rigours of the post-war economy curtailed such luxurious treatment straightaway, with a restriction to minimum services in 1919, and the wielding of the notorious 'Geddes Axe'; two years later. Sir Eric Geddes, and his finance committee, attacked the so-called Kempe-Fisher formula of grants automatically paid in relation to local decisions—it left, said Geddes, the Board of Education 'impotent'. Some of the severer cuts—raising the school starting age to six, for instance—were avoided and teachers creditably accepted a 5% salary cut (and there were others to follow in the 1931 economic crisis). 'Free' grammar school places became means-tested and re-christened 'special' places, while the early 30s saw school building and equipment programmes savaged by the slump. The 1936

Education Act tried to salvage this with improved building grants, but it was too late to be effective before the onset of the Second World War. In 1919/20 the leas spent £81,000,000, and in the fiscal year prior to that war they spent £139,000,000. The purchasing power of the pound was by then almost twice as much, which adds up to a depressing picture of government expenditure.

Now some of this must be explained by lack of commitment to education, just as the 1960s witnessed the opposite — a lively regard for the subject. Yet the inter-war years were otherwise a time of quite startling social changes. The motor car replaced the domestic servant as the status symbol of the gentlefolk; confectionary outlets multiplied more than twice over by 1938 by which time there were over 1,000 Boots branches. There was a radio in nearly every home; 10,000,000 punters sought a fortune on the football pools each week, and twice that number weekly searched for another kind of escape in the cinema. Education did not seem to keep abreast of these changes.

So perhaps more critical than the diffident attitude to education, as opposed to the vitality of other aspects of life, was the downbeat nature of the economy, and this serves to illustrate an important point about educational finance. The attendant disadvantage of education being centrally unified and financed was that it became that much more subject to the trials of the national economy. With the levers of national budget pulled and pushed to preserve that national economy, public education finance becomes a feature of fiscal policy, and is determined no longer by what might pass for educational justification. Of course, as the chapters on national policy suggested, the interlock of school and society is ever intimate, but, with massive sums involved in the complex mechanics of state budgeting, any educational considerations dropped further into the background.

This is obvious enough in terms of the strictures of the 30s depression, or of the ironing out of educational expenditure in the 70s, a tendency likely to grow during the 80s. What must also be realized is that the flamboyant expenditure of the 60s was a part of fiscal and not of educational policy. It has been convincingly argued that it was thought fiscally politic to invest in low-capital-cost jobs to maintain full employment. Unable or unwilling to find the investment for capital-intensive productive machinery, successive governments turned to the public services and created job openings by the thousand within them. Arguably, this had a disastrous effect on the economy, because it has meant the rundown of the 'marketable' sector of that economy, but that is another even sadder story. The upshot of pouring oodles of money into the education and other services was a shift from industry and allied activities.

Between 1961 and 1974 the percentage increase of jobs in the educational services was a staggering 76%, although the proportion of the population in receipt of education only increased 2% or 3%. Between 1961 and 1974 nearly 700,000 more employees were added to the education industry, making a total in mid-70s of 1,693,000 employed by leas, as opposed to 960,000 in the earlier year. That is an incredible 14% of the working population.

Perhaps the most terrifying feature of all is that, of the 1973 figure of 1,453,000 employed in education, only 51% are teachers and only 70% of those who work full-time actually teach. Many are in administrative posts or in lowly ancillary jobs, and the question must firmly be posed: did a 76% increase in employment in the education service lead to a substantial improvement in educational productivity?

That is the key general issue: the subjugation of education needs by national fiscal policy. Granted that, there are three subsidiary points to be raised about the current expenditure on education.

In the first place, and the preceding paragraphs are sufficient explanation, the bulk of educational funds is devoted to salaries. Of the monies directly spent by leas in 1977/78, £3,800,000,000 out of £6,300,000,000 — over 60% — was on salaries.

Taking merely the money spent directly on primary and secondary education, the proportion was as much as 83% on teaching and non-teaching salaries.

In the second place, once the taxes and rates are collected, the various formulae negotiated and the decisions made, there are certain variations in the expenditure from area to area which could be regarded as critical. For instance, and using 1974/75 figures, there seems to be a deal of difference between the exceptionally high ILEA expenditure of £575 per pupil, or Brent's £342, and Stockport's £241, although Stockport, well above the average in terms of 'A' level results and university entrants, might feel little need for anxiety. In fact the extremes are misleading, partly because of the higher salaries and other expenses of the London region, and indeed only five authorities in that year spent less than £250 and only ten more than £300. It might be argued that, technically, and through such devices as the Rate Support Grant and teachers quotas, we have a rough-and-ready equality of opportunity these days: as was pressed in chapter 8, the question is whether such uniformity of treatment is adequate.

In the third place, and in pursuit of that point about variation, the differentials are much wider as between age groups rather than as between areas. Unlike practically any other social service, education resources are available to an extraordinary degree of generosity for those least, rather than most, in need. The less gifted enjoy much shorter commons than their bright and clever fellows, and this is now very much taken for granted. It is worth recalling that the original intention of the public education service was to succour those who could not cope for themselves, just as the poor law or health insurance was provided for the poor and the impoverished sick. Universalizing the education service has paradoxically, turned it on its head. For instance, and these are 1977/78 figures, the annual expenditure on the 8% of the age range at university was £2,425 excluding grants, while the per capita expenditure on primary children—a 100% cohort—was no more than £324, 12% of the larger amount. For secondary pupils below the school leaving age it was £445, and for those above £801. Those who enjoy both the early privilege of nursery education and the later delights of higher education cost the state almost four times as much a those who plough the conventional five-to-16 furrow.

This is particularly ironic when it is remembered that, because of the social-class syndrome, the older 'aristocratic' monopoly of higher education and the new 'meritocratic' version are much closer in identity than once was thought. During the boom period of the 60s, when spending on higher education more than doubled from £160,000,000 to £360,000,000, when maintenance grants rose from £33,000,000 to £86,000,000, and when the percentage of 18-year-olds entering university jumped from 4% to 7% the 'non-manual' entrants (some 30% of the population) declined slightly from 73% to 70% and the 'manual' entrants (some 70% of the population) rose slightly from 27% to 30%. In other words, the children from middle-class homes more than held their own with working-class pupils. *Origins and Destinations* (A. H. Halsey, A. F. Heath, and J. M. Ridge, 1980) confirms tellingly this middle-class capacity to make preferential use of the public education system.

In an interesting calculation, Howard Glennester, the educational economist, examined carefully the increased expenditure of the 1960s. He concluded that the increase of expenditure on children from professional and managerial homes between 1962 and 1968 was 136%, but for children of skilled, semi-skilled and unskilled parents, it was 80% or less. Everyone saw a rise in expenditure, but the differences in the increase were enormous. This is a sobering thought, for there were optimistic cries in the air, as the pounds poured from the coffers and into the schools, about increased equality.

By way of summary, it might be added that, of the national education budget, the norm is for about 10% to be spent on universities, 30% on secondary schools, 20% on primary schools, and 0.33% on nursery schools, with the rest on administration, debt charges, capital works and other services. A mere 5% goes on the staff of the school-meals and milk service—facilities now under threat of heavy cuts.

Some of the global figures shown their paces here may seem a long way removed from the classroom, with the teacher busily struggling to make a lowly requisition fit what he feels to be the needs of the children. He may well feel that he has more in common with Sheffield Charity School's commercial exploitation of their pupils' ordure, and there have been recent examples of parents' associations finding funds for what would seem to be essential needs. However little the sums he handles, they flow or are stemmed because of the macro-finance of the nation. The particular funds are not made available primarily because of educational reasons, and teachers might also ponder on whether their deployment of such funds is evaluated according to educational criteria.

Essay subjects and seminar topics

1 A headteacher complained in a recent press statement that three children were sharing one hymn-book. But it's only for four minutes each day for a few verses of 'All the Past We Leave Behind' or 'Let Us with a Gladsome Mind'. Is the education service too extravagant? Visualize its budget cut by half. What system would you create on that (relative) shoestring?

2 'Getting value for money' is a much used exhortation. Devise a scheme, at a chosen educational level such as an infant school, for assessing whether the public money annually invested has been effectively used.

12 SERVICE OR SYSTEM

Nature, in giving you a son, presents you, let me say, a rude, unformed creature, which it is your part to fashion so that it may become indeed a man. If this fashioning be neglected you have but an animal still: if it be contrived earnestly and wisely, you have, I had almost said, what may prove a being not far from God.

Straight way from a child's birth it is meet that he should begin to learn the things which properly belong to his well-being. Therefore, bestow especial pains upon his tenderest years, as Vergil teaches. Handle the wax whilst it is soft, mould the clay whilst it is moist, dye the fleece before it gathers stains. It is no light task to educate our children aright. Yet think—to lighten the burden—how much comfort and honour parents derive from children well brought up: and reflect how much sorrow is engendered of them that grow up evilly. And further, no man is born to himself, no man is born to idleness. Your children are begotten not to yourself alone, but to

*your country, not to your country alone, but to God. Paul teaches
that women are saved by reason that they bring up their chldren in
the pursuit of virtue. God will straitly charge the parents with their
children's faults; therefore, except they bring up their little ones from
the very first to live right, they will share the penalty ... Such fathers
do not less wrong to their country, to which, as far as in them lies,
they give pestilent citizens.*

Erasmus, The Liberal Education of Children (1529)

Has an overwhelming centralization of English educational
administration underpinned with huge resources, solved the
country's educational troubles or do we still produce 'pestilent
citizens'? The first answer, of course, is that civilization is organic,
and the yardsticks change. Thus to be educated—as to be rich, or
healthy or even law-abiding—is a movable concept, applicable to
a given society at a given time. Certainly, as compared with a 100
years ago, the general tenor of feeling is that one requires a heftier
chunk, to put it no more courteously, of formal education than in the
1880s or earlier. Whether the quality is in as happy a condition as the
quantity is another matter; what is important is that education is
relative, like poverty or health. To be less educated than others, to
be, technically, 'ignorant' is, as was said of poverty, 'to be placed in a
particular relationship of inferiority to the wider society'. Inferiority
may be assessed in an amalgam of ways, including money, social
chances, cultural opportunities and status, and each of these, in part,
may be traceable to education.

In that sense, while it may be absolutely accurate to talk of an
overall increase in educational resources and facilities, and possibly
right to speak of an overall improvement in educational standards,
over the history of this nation's public education, it would be
incorrect to surmise that the relative provision of education
opportunity has been thoroughly equalized; indeed, it is arguable
that the gaps of relativity have not been closed overmuch. The
confused interlock of education with its socio-economic context,
already described in chapter 8, is one reason for this. Another
reason, touched on in the preceding chapter, is that education
rewards merit, however defined or arrived at, rather more liberally
than the opposite. More time and money is spent on increasing the
educational well-being of the already favoured than the less
favoured. In some ways this is not so eccentric an item of social
history: there are many who would argue that the National Health
Service is utilized with more benefit by the middle than the working
classes. In the *Lancet* of 15 June 1974, Professor Townsend explained
that between 1959 and 1963, 40,000 deaths of people in Social Class
V could have been avoided had there been equitable access to

National Health treatment. The health service, like the education service, began in an attempt to help those in need, developed into blanket coverage for everyone, and ended with the less needy reaping most benefit.

Of course, the argument runs that the state will prosper because of the development of the superior talent, and the borders between individual self-realization and the public good become hopelessly blurred. This must remain a moot point, and one that could lead to thickets of logic-chopping about whether, for example, the expensively educated director of the luxury product firm or the local dustbinman contributes more to the public good. Adhering temporarily to the issue of the individual good, there is little doubt that educational provision does not provide equal opportunity. Observe this sequence of success and failure as for an average sample of 100 children, 70 from working-class or manual and 30 from middle-class or non-manual homes, a reasonable microcosm of the nation.

	Start school	Reading Average or over at 7	Success in 11 plus	5 'O' levels	Sixth Form	Higher Education
MANUAL	70	47	8	6	4	1 or 2
NON-MANUAL	30	26	18	14	8	4 or 5

NB success in 11-plus may now read more legitimately, entry into comprehensive school top-stream.

In other words, equality and uniformity have been completely confused. An educational service offers a more helpful chance to those not impeded by other social ills and enjoying social habits which relate closely with those necessary for success in school.

This raises the question of whether a central authority can meet the real needs of equal opportunity. It appears as if the sovereign state can provide the mechanics of opportunity, but not the chemistry. It is capable, or so it would seem, of offering the same technical and legal chance to all its little clients. Every infant has an Oxbridge mortarboard in his satchel, just as, theoretically, the bishop's palace awaited every medieval serf. But the process is no more purely 'educational' for the youngster that it was purely 'theoretical' for the peasant. The sovereign state seems able to set the game of equality in motion but incapable of refereeing it so that equality can be guaranteed at the end. The liberal view might be that this is as much as the individual can expect—the freedom to whatever advantage he may make of his one educational chance, and that, in the general interest, this makes for the maximum efficiency of the state. But freedom is not automatically the same as equality.

One difficulty is the aspiration with which the notion of equal opportunity was and has been imbued. As with other social and economic features of modern life, a confusion exists between such radical or socialist idealism and centralism. It cannot be overemphasized that 'nationalization' is an administrative mode and not, per se, socialism. Many other nations, apart from ours (the French state of the sixteenth century, for instance) have known such centripetal forces. Thus it should not be assumed that central control inevitably improves the chances of equal opportunity. A further point is that central control inevitably improves the chances of equal opportunity. A further point is that centralization may have passed its peak and can do no more. The swings of legislative briskness and quiescence over the last hundred years might have led one to anticipate another dose of collectivism since 1964, but hopes have been dashed. The early Gladstonian period of the 1870s, the pre-1914 Liberals and the 'silent revolution' of the late 1940s were marked by giant steps in state invervention, with periods of consolidation in between, leading one to expect another radical burst during the Labour dominance of politics between 1964 and 1979. Although reforms, especially of a libertarian nature, have been attempted, central interference of a novel kind has not been a feature, and one must consider — as was hinted in chapter 3 — that the state's appetite is replete. This is not said unkindly, for the state's role has saved many from a parlous condition. The central state has not so much failed; rather is it a case that it can do no more. The outcrop of local and community groups is another pointer to the state's structural difficulty. In education these are the local parents' associations, the thrust for parent governors and the national bodies — like the Confederation for the Advancement of State Education or the Advisory Centre for Education which act, so to speak, in an extra-parliamentary manner to improve the education service. They are parallelled in other fields by patients' associations, tenants' associations, railway passenger associations and a hundred others, some focussing on a single issue — a motorway opening or a school closing — or adopting a generalized stance — on behalf of a school or a health centre.

They challenge the view that the supra-state can necessarily and at all times respond to the needs of its component parts. It is a converse of the notion that the state, at central or, in many respects, at local level, should be and is able to make decisions affecting citizens, without those citizens being privy to the decision-making process. At the school level it involves both choice of which school and thereafter choices about what sort of teaching or subjects a pupil might enjoy. It concerns the degree to which the education system has become standardized, a fear often expressed about large scale state enterprises. It is well-intentioned and superficially fair, but it is sometimes an insensitive response to need. It can become something of a blunt instrument. Compare this, educationally, with the kind of bureaucracy which decrees that every street should be cleaned once a week—irrespective of those which require sweeping every day or alternatively once a fortnight.

The Victorian idea of what a school should aim to do is an aspect of this standardization of treatment. It is connected with both the Victorian view of their social institutions, such as schools (see chapter 19) and the objective of education as defined by teachers (see chapter 18). *In toto*, the school and its organizers, be they officials, teachers or governors, have been imbued with strong characteristics of a civic, political, social and economic kind, often with religious overtones and even military undertones. And it has been the school's business, in the minds of many over the years, to produce appropriate initiates for the nation, conceived along the lines of those characteristics.

This might most clearly be stated in an industrial or a martial analogy, which is entirely apposite for much of English education over the last 150 years. Either the school leaver may be seen as the 'product' the finished article manufactured as near as possible to the school and the nation's blueprint, or as the 'trained soldier', who, having completed his basic drill, is prepared for the battle of life. Thomas Arnold could be regarded as the master cutler or the regimental sergeant major, according to personal choice, but there have been thousands of teachers, and probably millions of parents, who have, if only by implication, viewed the pupil as a combine of raw material and raw recruit. They have established and supported a process to enable an industrial-cum-military transformation to occur. It is indeed arguable that all education systems from the dawn of civilization have had this in common: namely the object of moulding youngsters in the shape demanded by the host society.

That may still be the case. Present day British society is pluralistic and open-ended, tolerantly eschewing racial, religious, political and sexist discrimination and valiantly embracing the virtues of individualism and, in moral and ethical terms, a fair degree of relativism. It is reasonable to suggest that, because of the inevitable time-lag between a change in society's character and the consequent alignment of its service institutions, schools and colleges are not quite up to date with this. They preserve a product-orientated regime, at the behest, it must quickly be added, of public as well as teachers. The gap between the reality of society and the actuality of the school produces something of a dual standard. For instance, although only 5% or 6% of the public can be persuaded to attend an act of worship weekly, as opposed to much higher figures years ago, all children, unless conscientious objections are raised, are required to attend a daily act of worship and receive a weekly period of religious education. This is not an argument about the rightness or wrongness of either: it is an instance of the chasm between what society preaches for its schools and what it practises itself.

The philosophic dichotomy of the school has been present in Britain since the time of the Reformation. The belief current since that time in man's independence and his right to seek individual salvation has balanced, not always easily, with the belief that man had to kow-tow to authority. It is reflected, for instance, in the writings of Erasmus. This has been particularly acute in schools, especially of late, where the desire to wean children toward an adult life of free decision-making clashes with the desire to preserve the authority of the home, the school and, of course, the state. Nonetheless, there seems to be a growing feeling that education should be more child-centred and more responsive to the realization of individual needs. Even this trend might have two sides: over against the view that children should be nurtured to emerge as original and unique human beings is the view that, because children are basically dissimilar, a child-centred approach, adjusting methods to such dissimilarities, is a more efficient way of producing a roughly similar 'product' at the end.

To project the commercial metaphor, the demand for a more individualized provision of education, stemming from whatever source, conceives of education as a service rather than a system. It conceives of the children and, by proxy, their parents as the users or consumers of this service. It expects them, as customers, to recieve a flexible and personal service. They are the users of a public service rather than the potential products of a nationalized industry.

Much of this concerns the professional attitudes of teachers, the anxieties and aspirations of parents and the general sentiments of the public. Fundamentally, however, it concerns the nature of the state and its relationship with the individual. Is a super-state, such as ours, able to provide a customer-based service of unimaginable variety and elasticity, or must it ever be shackled by officious pressures to be standardized and systematic? The future of the state education machine may well depend on whether it can shift from being a system, with products, to being a service, with customers.

Essay subjects and seminar topics

1 Many people believe that children in school should be treated at most times as individuals; some people believe they actually are. What are the chief practical obstacles to such an approach?

2 Conduct a brief survey of either another state education scheme—the French, the American, for example—or another

British public organization—the National Health Service, British Rail, Social Security, the Post Office, for example. To what extent is it 'system' and to what extent 'service'?

LOCAL GOVERNMENT

13 LOCAL CONTROL

'Politics', Samothrace insisted, 'is the pox that rots society'. He spoke of Athens. 'But it was politics and nothing else, with its sterile debates in the forum which brought Athens down. And Demosthenes, the last saviour of his country, was driven to poisoning himself...'

Mouraille claimed that communities, like bodies, may be ill, comparing the laws to old wives' remedies and coups d'etat to surgical operations. It is sometimes possible to prolong the life of a body by mutilating it, but death will be on the watch for it.

Tafardel rebuked the negative quality of this wisdom. 'Where, then' he asked, 'do you stand on society?'

'I am one of the ruled', Mouraille answered tranquilly: 'it would be wrong to increase the growing number of people who are trying to rule the rest...'

'The government of men' he (Samothrace) said, 'is simply a long alternation of two systems, always the same—the regime of force, and that of liberty. The former always ends in bloodshed, the latter in decay which is why man constantly changes from one to the other. Men can tolerate neither tyranny nor liberty for very long.'

Gabriel Chevalier, *Clochemerle—Babylon* (1954)

The development of local government's connection with education is the counterpart to that of the state's. It is the other side of the bipartite medallion by which most British public services are operated. It is, equally, the story of a gradually more rational, at least in managerial terms, and indubitably more expensive set of administrative mechanics. The narrative covers a comparatively shorter period. The dominance of the churches locally and the dormancy of the state nationally, coupled with the lethargy and ineffectiveness of much that passed for local government, meant that its involvement with education dates back little more than a hundred years, whereas the state has attempted, with varying success, to influence education for much longer. It is true that Liverpool experimented with 'corporation' schools from the 1820s, that Boards of Guardians exerted some control over workhouse schools and that the Society for the Promotion of Christian Knowledge had earlier worked in concert with local committees. But no national formula existed for local governmental action, and for two broad reasons: a lack of commitment to the idea that education, like law and order or highways, might validly be regarded as a public duty; and a lack of organizational equipment to deal with it were it so judged.

Particularly after the 1835 Municipal Corporations Act, which effectively reformed the apathetic and often corrupt governance of English towns, these feelings began to change: in places like Manchester and Birmingham there was the belief that education not only should but now could be organized by local government. Manchester, 'the shock city of the 1840s', in Asa Briggs' succinct phrase, was in the van of a movement to establish public education completely on a local as opposed to any form of national base. A whole series of bills, including a celebrated Manchester and Salford Education Bill in 1852, were mooted as test-cases for a system entirely dependent on the rates, but they all came to grief, because of religious opposition and parliamentary vacillation. Out of these efforts and the formation of various associations came the National Education League, centred on Birmingham, and, slowly, from about 1850 on, the mood changed, so that by 1870, some form of legislation for elementary instruction under local supervision became highly likely.

It was no accident that the large towns were at the forefront of the debate. The euphoria of the 1851 Great Exhibition declined into the dismay of the Paris Exhibition of 1867, as foreign competition began to assail Britain's proud role as the world's workshop. Richard Cobden, the famous Manchester politician and free trader, warned 'I don't think it is safe for us to be the most ignorant Protestant nation on earth...the very security, the very trade, and the progress of the nation depend not so much in the contest of arms as on the rivalry in the sciences and the arts which must spring from education.' British goods—'slovenly intruded heaps of raw materials mingled with rusty iron', according to one trenchant critic—were being outsold in the colonies by American goods, and inventions like the sewing machine and the automatic reaper began to pour out of the United States. Like coals to Newcastle, Belgian steel girders were imported into Sheffield and Birmingham engineering companies were sustained by American screws.

The economic anxieties of the age (some of them strangely familiar to modern ears) were keenly felt in the industrialized towns where local government was at its most thrustful. Their enterprising merchants, visiting, for instance, Germany, felt that the elementary schools there (systematically organized on parish and department, that is, local area, lines) provided for a labour-force skilled enough to handle delicate mechanical and clerical tasks and laid a basis for higher-grade technical studies to equip a pool of foremen and other supervisors. These towns were growing in confidence about local government, as, for example, they embarked, with conspicuous success from the 1840s, on the massive installation of water supply, sewerage and improved roadways in their localities, and were beginning to think in terms of libraries, parks and cemeteries as well.

They were, of course, pressed as much by necessity as they were motivated by sentiments of pride in the well-being of their home town. People sick because of inadequate public health facilities could not work in the factories to earn money to spend in the shops, while poorly-lit, badly made and refuse-littered streets incommoded the wheels of commerce. And, as regards education, it was precisely the large industrial towns which most witnessed the phenomenon of children neither at work nor school. In Birmingham, in 1866, it was claimed that of 8000 children aged three to 12, less than 1000 were at work, 4000 were at school and just over 3000 were at neither. As the Manchester Education Aid Society said of workless, school-less youngsters in 1866, 'without order of schooling, continuous labour and sober thought are alike impossible to them'. Once more the social worry of indolent children wandering the streets is to the fore, and it is a worry manifest in the police records of the large towns.

Part of Forster's 'hard compromise' of the 1870 Act was the idea of popularly elected School Boards in areas where there were deficiencies in provision. These were voluntarily established, with compulsion as a second-phase resort, and, inevitably, School Board coverage was not uniform or consistent. they were based on parish and borough boundaries, which made for enormous variations in size, from huge teeming cities like Liverpool to the tiniest village with one school. Forster could not utilize the existing parish vestries which, unlike the boroughs, were still unreformed, and had to fall back on this *ad hoc* procedure. Not that it was unusual, for the Victorians tended to opt for single purpose authorities, like Local Boards of Health, Highways Boards, Boards of Guardians and Burial Boards. As they acted to resolve some key problem, that tended to erect a novel agency, not least because of radical suspicions of the slothful existing machinery. Cumulative voting for a School Board membership of between five and 15 was granted every rate-payer, including women. There were often sectarian and political squabbles, not appeased by cumulative voting., In the notorious example of Birmingham the Tories gained control by concentrating votes on eight candidates, whereas the Liberals spread their support wastefully over 15 candidates. In other places—Liverpool is an example—compromise among the religious factions succeeded in avoiding an election at all, as each nominated an agreed number of candidates. Half the Boards had to be established compulsorily, and many Board members were keen to restrict positive action, usually in order to keep down the rates.

Nonetheless, in the 30 years of their history, 2511 School Boards were formed, under whose auspices 20,000,000 people lived. 790 School Attendance Committees, established, oddly, under the aegis of Urban Sanitary Authorities and Poor Law Unions, catered for the remaining 9,000,000 of the English and Welsh population. In effect, there was a roughshod uniformity from the viewpoint of procuring compulsory attendance at school. By 1899 a quarter (5,500) of the 'inspected' schools were Board Schools and almost a half (2,500,000) of the 'inspected' pupils studied in them. School Boards raised about £5,000,000 from the rates, in addition to the £9,000,000 distributed both to voluntary and Board Schools by the state. The move toward compulsory attendance was marked by aggravation. Soon after the passage of A. J. Mundella's 1880 Act, which effectively ensured obligatory attendance, as many as 1200 sets of bye-laws had been accepted. The Liverpool School Board set the pace with an average of a 100 imprisonments and 500 fines each year for non-compliance with the regulations. Truancy, as an illegal act, was born and parents, wishful of some income from their children, and employers, such as farmers desirous of casual, seasonal labour, could be as opposed to the new draconian laws as children, eager to escape the rigours of the three 'R's.

The 1870 Act was a piece of Liberal legislation, much hated by the Conservatives and their allies in church and shire. It was the cities, like Manchester, Nottingham, Birmingham, Sheffield, Bradford and Leeds, where heavy pockets of Liberal support, along with the commercial and nonconformist interests, applauded the Act. It was to be a classic precedent. The first entanglement of local government in education signalled political confrontation, a syndrome which has dogged educational management from then until the comprehensivisation quarrels of the last two decades. The swiftness of the boroughs to adopt School Board reforms contrasted with the dilatoriness of the Tory dominated rural districts, where, to be sure, the difficulty was less acute. The London School Board soon built or had transferred into its keeping 345 schools, and Leeds, by the 1880s, had opened 43 Board Schools.

As was described in chapter 10, rancour over the School Boards, no less than the rational objective of providing a saner scheme, led to that very contradictory statute, the 1902 Education Act. There is little doubt that the Conservatives distrusted the ambitious vigour and *parvenu* drive of the Boards, just as much as Fabian rationalists like Sydney and Beatrice Webb objected to their sporadic and unsystematic character. The Conservative local government reform of 1888 had established a uniform pattern of 62 counties or county areas (like the London County Council or the Yorkshire Ridings) together with almost as many county boroughs, that is, towns with over 50,000 inhabitants. These often lay uneasily side by side with the School Boards, and many were anxious to have education as an additional arrow in their quiver. From 1899 the counties had been allowed a penny rate for technical education and several set up Technical Instruction Committees: part of the animosity was founded in the Board's equal determination to support technical education. The case for making education part of the new multi-purpose authorities seemed overwhelming and thus, in 1902, this was accomplished, and so it has remained.

The uniformity created should not mislead one to consider the new leas in terms of equality. There was a world of difference between Lancashire's 2,250,000 population and 400,000 pupils and the Scilly Isles' 1,800 inhabitants and 250 pupils. Canterbury, an exception to the population ruling for County Boroughs, had 30,000 citizens and 6,000 pupils: a far cry from Birmingham's 1,250,000 populace and 200,000 pupils. The government had also to bow to fiery local feeling. The Counties and County Boroughs were called Part II authorities, with oversight of elementary and secondary education, but boroughs with over 10,000 or urban district councils with over 20,000 inhabitants were designated Part III authorities and permitted to watch over elementary education. There were over 200 of these, making 328 authorities in all, and, by this device, the ambit and personnel of several School Boards remained intact.

When one notes the continuing lack of pattern, the question is prompted as to whether a more efficient method might not have been a completion, perhaps with reforms, of the School Board pattern. The Board's range of scope was ludicrous, but they were often suited to local needs and their members were often single-mindedly devoted to education. Now education had to take its place in the queue with other services and was soon to become the largest cog in the local authority machine, with inevitable suspicions and envies. The replacement of one rate-levy for several may have led to a more co-ordinated financial management, but education had to join the stately quadrille of local government, with its lancers-like chains of proposals passing up, down and across a bewildering series of committees.

The 1944 Act did little to change the situation. It abandoned the Part III authorities, reducing the number of authorities from what had become 315 to 146. Local sentiments were still not to be denied.

The 1944 debates were most amenable and good-humoured, and one of the few flashes of indignation was sparked by the outraged Part III authorities. It was decided to have Divisional Executives to whom supervision of primary and secondary education could be delegated by the lea, albeit without any power to levy funds. The device of Excepted Districts was used, with sizeable borough councils acting as educational authority, under the aegis of a county lea and without fiscal power. Many of the mourning Part III authorities became such, and, although lacking in financial power, the growth of secondary education, and their subsequent rise in esteem, was usually sufficient compensation. Uniformity still remained somewhat theoretical: rating was a particular problem, with, for instance, a penny rate in Bournemouth raising three times as much as a penny rate in Gateshead.

But a chief pointer for consideration is the perseverance of the local potency. It is a good illustration of what geographers call the impetus of a start, with some districts struggling through from their initial status as School Boards, transmuting first to Part III authorities and then to Divisional Executives in 1944.

The 1974 reorganization of local government made education a function of metropolitan districts and shire counties, with a resultant fall in the numbers of leas to 104. It was argued that a given size of area was necessary for the deployment of local government services, and that a population of 300,000 was a rational optimum for education, bearing in mind other variables such as geographical size. As for population in the new, largescale units, this ranges from 181,000 in Barnsley to 1,000,000 in Birmingham, for metropolitan districts (which for several services come under the seven parent metropolitan counties, such as Merseyside or West Midlands) and from 111,000 in the Isle of Wight to 1,375,000 in Lancashire, for shire counties. Whatever the purported 'economies of scale' produced by this rationalization, it is doubtful whether, as far as the ordinary public is concerned, the lea is any less obscure and distant than before. Some reports suggest the reverse, claiming that the artificiality and largeness of the new authorities makes them too anonymous. Nor should the political aspects be forgotten. Local government reform was a Conservative measure, and many medium-sized County Boroughs, swallowed up by the surrounding shire, were normally of the opposite persuasion. Some administrative delegation, in the image of Part III authorities and Divisional Executives, has been retained via a divisional structure, sometimes based on shire districts, and, during the last months of the 1974-79 Labour Government there was talk of towns like Stoke, Nottingham and Southampton being given direct control once more over education.

The move away from the Victorian mono-purpose agencies to the cross-disciplinary local authorities of the twentieth century has long since been completed. More recently there have been endeavours at corporate management, with a closer cohesion of the varied services, and these have not been negotiated without friction, especially with education officers either resentful of or frustrated by the efforts of their colleagues. So great has become this educational component in local government that some have argued that the tendency of the state to encroach on these matters should be pursued to its logical if, for some, bitter end, and that the burden of education should be removed from the rates and accommodated entirely by taxation, with, presumably, a corresponding shift of political responsibility to the centre. However, the Conservative administration, elected in 1979, has shown some signs of reducing slightly the weight of central directives on matter such as buildings.

At the other extreme there are those who believe the trend should be reversed, and that the single-purpose authority should be re-introduced. John Mann, Secretary of the Schools Council and until then Sheffield's deputy chief education officer, argues convincingly in his *Education* for School Boards of seven to 13 members with populations of 20,000: 'their concentration', he writes, 'on one public service means they can devote more time to that service than members of multi-purpose authorities...they are responsive as well as accountable'.

There, in a nutshell, is the local goverment problem. It exists between the individual and the state, but, as the intermediate agency, is it the defender of the former or the co-belligerent of the latter? Many people, certainly in the nineteenth century, saw local authorities as a bulwark against an inquisitive and over-interfering state, but, conversely, many individuals might see local and central government amalgamated as the dreaded 'them' of officialdom. A significant consideration is obviously size and function, and it is apparent that the basic question about education and local government remains the same. What degree of autonomy should the local education authority enjoy apropos both state and other local governmental features, and what is a viable size for such an operation? Single-purpose or multi-purpose; small or large; independent of or dependent on the state—these are the three key issues.

Essay subjects and seminar topics

1 The difficulties of equating the strategies of large-scale and efficient organization with the tactics of political identification and localized action seems in local government terms, so far to have foxed the English. What do you consider to be the most

realistic outcome or next step in the development of local educational administration?

2 Selecting your home or a nearby local education authority, trace back its administrative lineage and off-shoots to 1870, particularly noting any conservation of personnel and internal organization behind the changes of labels.

14 ADMINISTRATIVE PROCREATION

In many respects an education service is a microscom of the local authority as a whole, and its management problems are similar to those of the local authority. Some of the problems are noted below:

Size: *the Sheffield education service spends over £30,000,000 a year and has 14,000 employees.*

Diffuseness: *300 separate institutions.*

Multipurpose: *embraces meals, health, psychological, welfare and careers services.*

Ill-defined aims: *qualified manpower, individual fulfilment, good citizens, development of society.*
Few measurable objectives.

No clear lines of accountability: *DES and LEA, church and state, LEA and school, Education Committee and governors.*

Internal departmentalism: *Schools, Special Services, Further Education, Youth Employment, Adult, Youth.*

Management in the Education Service: Challenge and Response,
An occasional paper of the Society of Education Officers, 1974

The operational balance between central and local government is deliberately contrived so that parliament and the secretary of state propose—by enactments, regulations and circulars—and the local education authorities dispose i.e. what actually occurs is decided by the local education committees. Consultation takes place, principally through CLEA (the Council of Local Education Authorities) which has two components, one representing the counties (the Association of County Councils) and the other the metropolitan districts (the Association of Metropolitan Authorities). Much of this consultation is, as a result, dominated by the prevailing climate of party politics; indeed, unless one party has a majority in both branches, no united front can be presented to central government, unless, of course, the parties happen to agree on the relevant issue.

The existence of these powerful organs of local government, of whom few ratepayers have probably heard but whose voice is carefully heeded before legislative action is attempted, is a pertinent reminder of the bureaucratic levels society now tolerates.

The local education authorities encompass a wide range of services for people of all ages, including meals, careers and educational psychological guidance, and the acute degree of specialization (for instance, in the needs of handicapped children or the teaching of English as a second language) is now quite elaborate. It is a complex set of mechanics, with a complex chain of command both internally and, through the national hierarchies of the AMA, the ACC and CLEA, externally. It is extremely expensive, as chapter 11 maintained, and it has become extremely bureaucratic, in the sense of power or, at least, tasks being in the hands of officials.

The numbers involved are themselves daunting. Since the 1870s the total of local government employees (like the total of central government employees) has grown remorselessly. Between 1880 and the end of the last century the numbers employed in 'general and local government' rose from 106,000 to 198,000, and thus almost doubled. The upward rate has proved inexorable. Between 1961 and 1974 central government employees increased over 9%, from 524,000 to 575,000, but local government employees leapt dramatically from 1,755,000 to 2,697,000, a staggering increase of almost 54%. The increase in educational employment was from 960,000 to 1,693,000 over that period, inclusive of non-lea services, such as the universities.

The actual local education authority figure of employees for 1978 was some 1,385,000 of whom 640,000 were part time. Only 676,000 of these were teachers or lecturers. Of the part timers 497,000 were *not* teachers, as opposed to 143,000 who were, that is 29%. Many of these are, of course, employed in services like school meals, as well as in administration proper, but, all in all, it seems to need as many again to keep the teaching force in the field. Translate the whole of this into a pupil: employee ratio, and it appears that leas employ approximately one worker, full or part time, to every six or seven pupils.

With the average sized local authority responsible for a budget of some £30,000,000, with probably a central adminstrative staff of 300 or more, and with a major committee and several sub-committees for which to cater, the normal lea presents a picture of official life very close to a large business in character, like an insurance company or merchant house. Although there is fierce and increasing competition from other services for local authority resources, the education committees control over half their authority's budget. This means they are most likely to assault from smaller rivals, such as social services or leisure and recreation departments, simply because the sizeable fraction invites the most envious eyes. In fact, not all that much of an education budget is variable. About 85% in any one year is bespoke: 65% on the salaries of teaching and non-teaching staffs, 15% on debt charges on capital loans borrowed years previously for building and the like, 5% on student awards, further education items and other bills that must be paid. A considerable amount of the service is statutorily laid down, and the costs must be met. This leaves 15% — and some estimates place the figure much lower — for teaching materials, like books and stationery, the maintenance of equipment and buildings, the cost of light and heat, and such matters as office administration and school transport. It is for this reason that, when cuts are in the offing locally, it is usually teaching materials and maintenance which are the first to suffer.

There is no doubt that the demands of the state for a most widespread set of services within the education sector, going far beyond the direct business of a group of children and a teacher in a classroom, have been a major cause of the increase in lea employment. More and more controls are established and more and more information is sought by central government, to the horror and consternation of local government. But, equally, there is no doubt that the fiscal laws described in chapter 2 have been at work encouraging, during the 60s particularly, huge increases in the number of staff. Again, there is also a snowball effect to be considered, what the administrative historian, Oliver Macdonagh, has called 'administrative procreation'. A fresh initiative, an extra officer or new sub-committee might require two or three clerical officers, who will need typists to prepare their documents, and juniors to run their messages, file and post the documents and make the tea:

Large fleas have small fleas upon their backs to bite 'em,
And small fleas have smaller fleas, and so on, ad infinitum.

Take Gloucestershire's outline of its education 'hemisphere', as it was entitled, just prior to local government reorganization. It was divided into three Programme Areas — Scholastic services, Vocational Assistance Services and Recreation and Leisure Service. Each area had four or six sections and each section was broken down into about half-a-dozen activities. The one, under Scholastic Services, marked 'Older Children' included such diverse activities as museums, short-term residential facilities, the school psychological service and school uniform grants. Such activities criss-crossed and overlapped with those in other sections to complete a bewildering mesh of formal action. Gloucestershire's is used as an example for its neatness: some lea administrative structures are not capable of such tidy description. The point is that leas have all adopted some such bureaucratic formula, and all teachers work for a complicated network of this kind. Especially since the advent of the rationalized lea pattern of the post 1974 period, both parents and teachers have complained about such complications and how difficult it is to trace a route through the system when some poser—teachers' pay for instance—has to be resolved. Conversely, there is a feeling that so complex an official format makes onerous demands on schools for returns and records of many sorts, so that paperwork begins to take over from teaching.

These homely illustrations should remind that bureaucracy is an emotive word, indicative of delay and procrastination. Strictly speaking, bureaucracy is government by officials, and like any other form of government it might be good or bad. For Max Weber, the famous sociologist who lived from 1864 to 1920 and who did much of the original analysis of the phenomenon, bureaucracy meant efficient and rational adminstration. It was, for him and others, the reverse of the muddling, amateurish and corrupt management of yesteryear, and, to be fair to bureaucracy, the promotion of officials by talent, and not by patronage and favouritism, has probably happened more frequently (but certainly not exclusively) under bureaucratic management. Weber saw bureaucracy as the 'mechanical' approach to organization, a parallel to the introduction of machines in the economy. It is the impersonal nature of bureaucracy which is its chief virtue. It is, at best, systematic, specialized and expert, unmoved by emotion and essentially public in character. It is not idle to state that, if we wish to sustain a massive system of public services, like education, health, the post office and the rest of the state's superstructure, then bureaucracy is absolutely necessary.

The difficulty lies, as ever, in the excess of virtue becoming vice. Any bureaucracy is prone to the diseases of being oversystematic and restrictive, specialized to the point of atrophy, dehumanized and unimaginative, and secretive and cautious into the bargain. In the longer term, this could result in bureaucracy being the master rather than the servant of the people, and many fear this has already happened in local education and elsewhere in modern life. Weber (who was not unaware of these hazards) knew that 'bureaucracy inevitably accompanies mass democracy', because only impersonal governmental machinery can provide equal public treatment. Paradoxically, it is, by that very token, its most dangerous and wily enemy, for the expert 'bureaucrat', with security of tenure, may easily outflank and control the lay 'democrat', subject to electoral scrutiny. Weber himself noted that bureaucracies tended to preserve themselves, not least by hiding knowledge to obviate criticism. In

Leslie Chapman's *Your Disobedient Servant* (1978) it is suggested that, subsequent to the Fulton Report of 1968 on the Civil Service, Whitehall successfully managed to adopt those recommendations which were favourable, like better conditions, and avoid those which hinted at closer inspection and oversight.

At the lea level the dichotomy is clearly to be seen. A democratically elected education committee, vulnerable to public opprobrium and the ballot-box, part-time and perhaps inexperienced, is very much at the behest of its highly professionalized staff of education officers, advisers and administrators. They control the supply and content of the information to the committee and the public, they organize the frame of reference for meetings, they adopt their own jargon and managerial codes, and, day by day, they make crucial executive decisions. It is as if the 'democratic' aspect is nineteenth-century in style, with its rather musty series of committees and sub-committees and arcane sub-parliamentary procedure, while the 'bureaucratic' aspect is twentieth-century in character, with its high degree of management technology. Others, more gloomily cynical, might think both are reminiscent of the Czarist Russia of Gogol's *The Inspector-General*, with squabbling politicoes vieing with incompetent officials as to who might produce the greatest amount of inefficiency, corruption, indolence and general confusion.

The democratic-bureaucratic balance is not, of course, universally unattainable, and, where the alert, bright education committee member is in a sound working relation with the dedicated, compassionate education officer, all could be well. Often, however, the staff rooms of today contain teachers ready to complain with equal lack of charity about the arrant pomposity of councillors and the meddling stupidity of officials.

One must try to judge in terms of output. One must raise questions about the effectiveness of the system in terms of the pupils and students, asking whether they receive an improved educational service as a result of so ingenious a bureaucratic arrangement. Granted the expansion of educational officialdom and back-up support since the late 1950s, if would seem reasonable to inquire whether educational standards, however defined, have risen. Many commentators would ponder whether, in fact, they have, although the difficulties of measuring output in the education service are well rehearsed. Sometimes officials will be heard bemoaning this fact, but it can and does work also to their advantage. With no recognizable yardsticks, like making a profit or producing a certain quantity of a certain product, the bureaucrat is that much more protected from the buffets of criticism, and, as he operates a wellnigh monopolistic service, there is an evident risk of educational officialdom becoming evermore self-contained and impregnable, self-fulfilling its own predictions of how it should proceed. 'Under normal conditions the power position of a fully developed bureaucracy is always', said Max Weber, 'overtowering'.

Fortunately, there are many education committee members and education officers who are motivated primarily by the desire to provide the children in their authority with a decent schooling. Whether they are or will remain in the ascendant is problematic, and whether, if they succeed, they will be capable of reining the local governmental leviathan is equally questionable. It is not the melodramatic threat of the bloodcurdling, chilling managerial machine, enslaving and shackling the people, which is the risk. That would be putting it too colourfully. It is the more humdrum hazard of an over officious, uninventive, dilatory administration which is the chief risk in educational circles today. When the commissar inquired of the East European peasant about the potato harvest, he was told that there were sufficient potatoes to reach from mother earth into the very lap of God. The commissar rebuked the peasant. 'Comrade peasant', he said sternly, 'it has been proved by the cosmological scientific application of the Marxist-Leninist principles of dialectical materialism that there is no God'. 'No, comrade commissar', replied the peasant simply, 'and there are no potatoes'. For potatoes, substitute education.

Essay subjects and seminar topics

1 'Developing democratic methods for governing bureaucracies is, perhaps, the crucial problem of our age'.

Peter Blau in *The Dynamics of Bureaucracy* (1963)

Discuss such possible methods in relation to local education authorities.

2 'Schools are subject to the bureacratic faults of over officiousness, secrecy, undue prudence and straitlaced adherence to unnecessary rules'. Analyze any cases you are aware of or have experienced, using the bureaucratic-democratic formula as a guide.

15 ACCOUNTABILITY

O Cromwell! Whither art thou aspiring? The word is already given out amongst their officers, that this nation must have one prime Magistrate or Ruler over them; and that the General hath power to make a law to bind all the Commons of England; This was most daringly and desperately avowed at White-hall; and to this temper the Court-officers are now a-moulding, he that runs may read and fore-see the intent, a New Regality! And thus by their Machiavilian pretenses, and wicked practizes they are become masters and usurpers of the name of the Army and of the name of the Parliament; under which Visors they have levell'd and destroyed all the Authority of this Nation: For the Parliament indeed and in truth is no Parliament, but a Representative of Class of the Councel of War; and the Councel of War, but the Representative of Cromwell, Ireton, and Harrison; and these are the all in all of this nation; which under these guises and names of Parliament, Army, General Councel, High Court, and Councel of State, play all the strange pranks that are played.

Richard Overton *The Hunting of the Foxes* (1649) a Leveller tract

The Levellers were not the first and they were certainly not the last group to be anxious—in their case with good reason—about the 'New Regality' of central power. They were, in action, *petit bourgeois* decentralizers rather than populist egalitarians, and, as such, it is not too fanciful to see the parental movement in England and Wales in the same tradition. In democratic terms, the education system is, technically, the people's system: they pay for it and use it. Morally, it is their children who suffer the slings and arrows of outrageous state education. And yet, as has been outlined in the previous chapters, the 'masters and usurpers' have taken unto themselves great powers, and are more than likely to 'play all the strange pranks that are play'd.'

The suspicion of centralized and bureaucratic power traverses the political spectrum. The far left see the state school as a capitalist instrument of repressive tolerance, gentling the masses, preparing the factory fodder and protecting the privileges of the élite. The right see the state schools as social engineering works, suppressing the liberties of the individual and winning the world for socialism. The truth probably lies somewhere in the middle, with the state, society and the school locked in a baffling cyclic process, and the school controlled, like many other institutions of the age, by an occasionally heavy-handed officialdom. What bothers most parents is strictly educational, and often relates to this circular process. It concerns what they believe to be their inability to influence or guide the manner in which they feel their children should be raised. It may be the wrong reading method they think is being used, or a too informal approach to maths that is being attempted, or an unhelpful set of options that is on offer for examination purposes. In short, the parent and in time the pupil or student, occasionally wish to question the pedagogic treatment they are receiving. At that point, they often find the school is not accountable to them, but to itself, and, back beyond that, first to the local education authority and then the Department of Education and Science. Here the quarrel, if quarrel it be, is not only with the bureaucracy at local authority level, but with the school in its professional 'visors'. To some degree, this analysis overlaps with the description in chapter 18 of teachers' professional status, and the relation of the teacher to the parent—but the issue of accountability, of judging whether or not the school is acting in the interests of its pupils and their families, concerns officials and elected members, as well as teachers.

The urge to obtain more influence at the field level of a public service is not restricted to education. It is probably more advanced there than in, say, the health service, council housing or the social services, perhaps because it is a service more regularly used by the mass of people. There are parents' associations, parent-governors in many schools, and a number of national bodies, like the National Confederation of Parent Teacher Associations, and there is even a National Union of School Students. These are active in attempting to enforce parental and pupil rights to have a say in what schools should do and how they should be organized. They suffer, however, from two major inhibitions.

In the first place, the public authorities, central and local, are subject, as they rightly claim, to the vote. Powers may be delegated to a school board of governors, but the sovereignty of central government remains unimpaired. What parliament or the lea, within its terms of reference, wills, they may un-will. The MP and the local councillor might argue that they represent the users of the education service, so what need have they for further ornate political mechanics? In the second place, as we noted in the last chapter, people feel disquieted by the divorce of the men in the street from the men in the corridors of power. The lack of contact and consultation between the providers and receivers of public services in this country fosters the belief that representative democracy cannot cope with the present scale of public activity. There are signs that central and local bureaucracies have taken over huge areas of decision-making that immediately affect the parent and pupil, and that these, the customers, are no more perplexed than their guardian angels, the MPs and the councillors. In any event, it is the delivery point of the service that matters most to the people, and, even where the peoples' representatives have not been disarmed by the depredations of bureaucratic man, it is precisely at the micro-level that few or no mechanisms exist. It is often at the very point of impact, where suddenly his child's destiny seems in the balance, that the user, the parent, is denied access to the consultative process. He may vote for and lobby his MP to increase expenditure on education; he may vote for and canvass a councillor to build a new comprehensive school—but when the expensive, new school tells him his son can't do zoology 'O' level, he abruptly finds himself without rights and unrepresented.

Looked at from another angle, government finds itself in a hapless dilemma. It must provide and maintain the education service, and then it must assess it and arbitrate upon it. Accordingly, an education committee locally or parliament nationally is asked both to provide the most extravagant or the cheapest service, dependent on whether one wears a parent/pupil or a tax/rate-payer's hat. It may be that the task of central and local government should be defined more clearly in managerial and fiscal terms. They represent the citizenry in their fund-raising role and should perhaps organize the services, such as education, as economically as is concomitant with efficiency, leaving the assessment and response to the users. This, however, they show little signs of doing, and the exploration of accountability of schools to their consumers has tended to split down two rather different avenues; choice of schools and local control of schools.

At its simplest, those who favour choice claim that, if parents are able to select the school they prefer, this would act as a monitor on schools, forcing unpopular ones to adapt or die. This has become an especially lively issue at a time of tumbling rolls, for many schools could be expendable. To those who complain that tax investment and other resources would be lost, Rhodes Boyson, a doughty advocate of choice, has fairly countered that 'this is a strange argument, for there is little satisfaction for the taxpayer in paying the running costs of a school that parents don't like!' Nevertheless, local authorities are bound to be discomforted by what they see as the impracticability of such schemes, for they might not know from year to year which schools might prove to have superior or inferior box office appeal. They prefer to have some firm control, on PALs (Planned Admission Limits).

To some extent the notion of wide-open choice conflicts with the neighbourhood or zoning principle, believed by many to be preferable, in so far as the school can endeavour to work for and serve, and, in turn, be supported by its host community. It is argued that the loyal partner is a pleasanter concept that the watchful client, constantly threatening to move his or her custom. Several leas, in a golden mood of compromise, attempt to win the best of both worlds, giving parents an absolute first-choice of a place in their neighbourhood school, but with an opting-out clause (normally taken up by less than 10% of parents) to use another school if it so be wished.

At its extreme, the choice argument becomes commercial, with the urging of the 'voucher' idea. The voucherist argues that, by providing everyone with a basic coupon to trade in at the chosen school, competition for funds would result in more consumer-conscious schools, responsive to the public will. The triple virtues of greater choice, greater variety and greater efficiency would, it is claimed, result from the operation of the market in education. Most voucherists do not deny the right of parents to supplement that basic voucher from their own pockets nor hide the fact that private schools would gain enormously from such a device. Only through the naked control of funds, it is pressed, will parents and pupils exert adequate influence. Alum Rock, California, was the scene of the most celebrated 'voucher' experiment and judgements vary as to its efficiency. There have been moves to introduce a 'voucher' scheme in Kent.

The anti-voucherist suggests that physical and geographic constraints of educational provision would make choice well-nigh impossible. Schools would adopt postures—the traditional school, the *avant garde* school—and, as happens in commerce, gull the customers into acquiescence. There is a suspicion that choice, and particularly by vouchers, is a souped-up version of educational apartheid, with those from areas of low population, or on low incomes, or otherwise disadvantaged, unable to exert valid choices.

On the other hand, the proponents of decentralization place their faith in running rather than choosing schools. They propose that the public ownership of schools may be delegated right to the delivery-point of the service, namely, the school itself. Its most notable and clear-cut exposition is in the Taylor Report of 1977, whose proposed governing institution for schools is a classic formula of devolved management. It recognized that the parents, and, as appropriate, the pupils have an interest as consumers, that the teachers have an interest, as professionals or as the labour-force of the school, and through its councillors, the lea has an interest, as the management element, representing the rate-payers who are funding the school. It proposed, in fact, that a fourth element—local community delegates—should be added to form the now famous consensus of quarters. It is interesting that it has been counter attacked by local governmental and party politicians, keen to preserve political dominance on governing boards, even although political nominees on such committees have been subjected to much criticism for absenteeism, lack of commitment and other sins.

There is also a distinction drawn between structure and function. There have been moves to include parents and teachers on very many governing bodies in the majority of local authorities: the Taylor Report was, in essence, a record of existing good practice. But very rarely have any such boards been allowed great or sufficient powers. Governing bodies usually operate within a narrow area of influence left them after the central and local authorities have made their dispositions. If matters such as staff appointments, budgetary allocations and curriculum oversight were devolved, then the move from representative democracy to popular democracy would be partway accomplished. There's the rub. Are we ready to shift from a situation in which we delegate our individual powers to representatives such as councillors or MPs to one in which we actually take the troubles and the decisions personally? Jeremy Bentham argued that, as far as possible, the interests of the governed and the governors should be identified—and the school organized primarily by teachers and parents in cooperation is a splendid example of this concept.

Not everyone is happy about the idea. The counter-argument is that the central and impersonal character of public authority has been necessary over the last century, to ensure that an equitable educational service could be mounted. It is a view emanating from the respectable theory that minors must be protected. This has been most trenchantly put by Frank Musgrove in a well-publicized statement: 'it is the business of education in our social democracy to eliminate the influence of parents on the life-chances of the young...the inequalities of parents are demonstrable...we have decided that children shall not be at the mercy of their parents. It is the business of a local education authority to see that they are not'.

In the autumn of 1979 the new Conservative administration published its Education Bill, which became law in 1980. It included measures to extend parental choice, with appeal tribunals (supposedly independent but likely to have heavy lea representation) to deal with unresolved cases, and to boost the notion of parent governors. Over time such enactments could formalize the position of the parent considerably.

But it is a salutary reminder that parents are *not* the consumers of education; it is the children who are the customers of the education service, and their parents stand proxy for them until they reach their years of discretion. It does not automatically follow that, when parents and teachers are agreed, the best interests of the pupils are necessarily served. The crux of the question, then, must remain: what system of school governance and accountability will satisfy the educational requirements of the child?

Perhaps there must always be what Vernon Bogdanor, fellow of Brasenose College and Conservative party educational pundit, calls a 'necessary tension'. 'Freedom', he has written, 'in the sense of freedom to buy and sell in an economic market, has always been restricted in modern democracies...It is not because of economic efficiency that some goods are removed from the competitive market, but rather because a democracy requires that certain rights be equally held and universally distributed. Instead of a simple choice between freedom and regulation there is a necessary tension between them, leaving the pragmatist the task of finding a balance between *laissez faire* evils and inefficient egalitarianism'.

Essay subjects and seminar topics

1 'If your employer issues you with luncheon vouchers, you may take your pick of numerous restaurants. There, you may eat a meal of your choice from a varied menu and, should you prefer the most expensive steak to the plain omelette and chips, you would be required to top up your voucher with some extra cash out of your pocket or purse'.
—John Izbicki, *Daily Telegraph* Education Correspondent,
defending a proposed voucher scheme for Kent schools (12 June 1978). How far is the restaurant/school analogy accurate?

2 In a recent opinion poll, in answer to the question, 'Who should help run state schools on a day to day basis?', teachers and parents scored about 80%, local councillors, older pupils and interested individuals from the local community about 30%, and nominees of political parties (the chief device for forming governing bodies) 6%. Discuss.

THE TEACHING PROFESSION

16 THE TEACHER

Bradley Headstone, in his decent black coat and waistcoat, and decent white shirt, and decent formal black tie, and decent pantaloons of pepper and salt, with his decent silver watch in his pocket and its decent hair-guard round his neck, looked a thoroughly decent young man of six-and-twenty. He was never seen in any other dress, and yet there was a certain stiffness in his manner of wearing this, as if there were a want of adaptation between him and it, recalling some mechanics in their holiday clothes. He had acquired mechanically a great store of teachers' knowledge. He could do mental arithmetic mechanically, sing at sight mechanically, blow various wind instruments mechanically, even play the great church organ mechanically. From his early childhood up, his mind had been a place of mechanical storage. The arrangement of his wholesale warehouse, so that it might be always ready to meet the demands of retail dealers—history here, geography there, astronomy to the right, political economy to the left—natural history, the physical sciences, figures, music, the lower mathematics, and what not, all in their several places—this care had imparted to his countenance a look of care, while the habit of questioning and being questioned had given him a suspicious manner, or a manner that would be better described as one lying in wait. There was a kind of settled trouble in the face. It was the face belonging to a naturally slow or inattentive intellect that had toiled hard to get what it had won, and that had to hold it now that it was gotten. He always seemed to be uneasy lest anything should be missing from his mental warehouse, and taking stock to assure himself.

Charles Dickens *Our Mutual Friend* (1864/5)

The Bradley Headstones of Victorian England were caught in a social trap between their middle-class betters and the working classes whom they served. Efforts to form a Registration Association of teachers so that they might be deemed a liberal profession proved abortive, in 1869, 1879, 1881 and 1890—and only the last endeavour even included elementary school-teachers. Teachers have had to be content with a second-rate professional status, inferior to law or medicine and, unlike those professions, they still have no overall institution such as a General Teachers' Council to pronounce on professional matters. In pay and social grading, teachers have long been, in the old-fashioned phrase, lower-middle class. For over a hundred years the great majority have been state patronees, without that distinction of being contractually or self-employed which is often the mark of the pukka profession, and only recently has the move toward a graduate profession been completed.

One reason for this is the substantial number of teachers, as opposed to the tighter, restrictive recruitment of other professions. There are today relatively few doctors and solicitors, compared with 468,000 (full-time and full-time equivalent) teachers. The growth of the teaching profession has been considerable. In 1870 there were 12,000 certificated teachers, 14,000 pupil-teachers (Bradley Headstone had his Charlie Hexam in *Our Mutual Friend*) and 1000 adult assistant teachers; totalling 27,000. By 1895 these figures were 53,000, 34,000 and—a colossal jump—28,000 respectively, totalling 115,000, a quadruple leap over the School Board period. Since the 1902 Education Act, the numbers of adult teachers have increased as follows, and prior to the huge increases of the 60s and 70s:

1902: 114,000, 1920: 170,000, 1950: 216,000, 1960: 269,000.

These figures have obviously kept pace with the rise in population and the amount of statutory education children have been obliged to undertake. They also reveal that pupil-teacher ratios have improved radically over the years. For instance, the pupil-teacher ratio in 1910/11 (when, following the 1902 Act it was possible to judge elementary and secondary schools together) was 36; by 1950 it was 27; and by 1980 it was 19. This is certainly light-years in educational method away from the Yorkshire log-book entry, which, after a virulent critique of a young teacher, added as an afterthought 'but perhaps some allowance should be made for the fact that he is only 13 and there are 87 in the class'. The halving of the pupil-teacher ratio since the 1900s is possibly the most notable achievement of English educational investment. It is that much more creditable when it is remembered that, prior to the 1902 Act when only elementary schools were state-aided, the pupil-teacher ratio was almost 50.

One other significant change occurred over the hundred or so years of direct state education. It became female-dominated, or, more rudely, as an oldish colleague told me on the first day of my own teaching career, 'hag-ridden'. Given that not uncharacteristic view, inside and outside schools, of women in the professions, this goes some way to explaining why teaching never approached those vocations which were strictly male confines. Whether the changing attitudes to sexism will alter this trait remains to be seen. In actual fact, teaching was never free from the chauvinist abuse of my erstwhile staff-room confrère. In 1870 half of the certificated teachers—like Miss Peecher, Bradley Headstone's opposite number in the adjacent girls' school—were women, but, by the 1920s, there were three women out of every five elementary teachers. The Great War played its macabre part. It slaughtered hundreds who taught or who might have taught, but more particularly, it slaughtered thousands of husbands and potential spouses. Many girls whose social gentility had or might have made them brides of the badly-mauled officer class turned in despair to teaching. The typical infant/junior school of the 30s (I quote my own as an example) had a widow as headteacher, supervizing eight middle-aged spinsters. There was even discrimination against married women, and tales abounded of wives wearing wedding rings about their necks to keep their guilty secret and their job. During the 60s, when teacher recruitment was inordinately boosted, may girls were attracted to teaching, if only temporarily. One estimate at that time suggested that the average teaching life of a female teacher was but four years. In 1963, 17,000 entered and 15,000 teachers left the profession. The proportions are now, overall, nearer a half, with the distaff side still predominating in the primary sector.

Some general outline of manpower employed in education may be gleaned from the following schedule for the year 1976/77:

Public Sector:
Full-time teachers and lecturers

Primary schools	238,000 ⎫	
Secondary schools	267,000 ⎬	505,000

Part-time teachers and lecturers
(full-time equivalents)   34,000

Other Public Sector:

(e.g. Further Education) & miscellaneous	121,000
Universities	33,000
Support staff (full-time & full-time equivalents)	479,000
Independent schools	28,000
Total	1,200,000

With the fall in pupil numbers, the figure for primary and secondary teachers combined is a little lower now at 468,000, but they amount in approximate terms, to over 40% of the full-time labour-force of education in England and Wales. (Incidentally, any deviation from the figure of 1,700,000 employees quoted in Chapter 14 is explained by these present figures being full-time or full-time equivalents as opposed to actual persons, full or part-time, employed).

To further the analysis, it should be stressed that approaching 500,000 teachers with a pupil-teacher ratio of 19 begins to look a little different when examined at classroom level. For instance, the distinction between primary and secondary pupil-teacher ratios is well-known. In 1977 it was 24 per qualified teacher in the former, and 17 in the latter, a considerable difference. In terms of size of classes taught, that meant just over 22 in secondary and just over 27 in primary schools; 13% of secondary and 35% of primary classes, with only one teacher in charge, still topped the 30 mark. There are also variations from authority to authority. In the same year the 'staffing standard' ranged, for primary schools, from Newcastle-upon-Tyne's 19.5 to Stockport's 27, and for secondary schools, from Harrow's 15 to Somerset's almost 19. Such variations, whilst seemingly slight, may make drastic differences to daily school organization. In considering these statistics, of course, one has to recall that some schools are neither primary nor secondary but, for instance, middle schools; that, with varying forms of organization, class size is not always a reliable indicator, and, especially in secondary schools, more teachers than in years gone by have shorter teaching timetables in order to undertake administrative and other functions.

With over 40% of the astronomic education budget devoted to teachers' salaries and with such large numbers involved, it is little wonder that teachers have organized themselves into unions or associations. The National Union of Elementary Teachers was formed in that *annus mirabilis* of education, 1870, and the 'elementary' was dropped in 1889, and this still remains the largest of the teaching associations, although there are others represented on the Burnham Committee for the discussion of teachers' salaries and conditions of service. The Assistant Masters Association (1891) and, interestingly, seven years earlier, the Assistant Mistresses Association were, for example, established chiefly for secondary teachers. The National Association of Schoolmasters/Union of Women Teachers is another important and vociferous union, while, since 1890, headteachers have had their own organization. The fissionable nature of teacher unionism reflects both the variety of work carried out by teachers, and, more meaningfully, the unease teachers experience with the concept of vocational solidarity.

There is much vagueness about whether teachers are in 'unions' of 'associations', whether, in fact, they are skilled tradesmen or qualified professionals; all illustrating the rather uncomfortable social position of teachers.

Teachers themselves are confused in such role-plays. It is, in part, psychological. The teacher spends his or her working day with the consumers; the miner, conversely, spends his with other miners, and the relative coherence of strike action by the two groups is noticeable. It is partly physical. It takes a long time for a teacher's strike, like, for instance, a postman's strike, to take effect and cause havoc, over against the almost instant chaos resultant from industrial action by miners or electrical workers. Nevertheless, the basic premise remains. Teacher organizations have the wishes of their members first at hand, and it would be mistaken of the public to expect teacher unions to put the consumers' interest before their own. It is not easy, in terms of imagery, to think of Mr Bloggs, marking, for his thirtieth year, the Latin unseens of some country grammar school fourth form, or Miss Snooks, briskly supervizing the sand and water play of a flurry of five-year-olds, alongside a flying picket of Yorkshire miners. They do not seem the stuff, whatever their other meritorious qualities, of which the Shrewsbury Six were made. But it would be wrong to mistake the form for the substance. Technically, the teachers, like the power workers, the miners and the postal workers, constitute the well-organized labour-force of a public monopoly.

The teachers are well-organized at national, local and school level, with district branches of the powerful national bodies, seats on education committees and governing bodies, staff associations in many schools, and a network of consultation at all levels. They have obtained very adequate salaries for what, minimally and recognizing the extra hours and days worked by many teachers, are excellent hours, with splendid holidays, a sufficient pension and, what is the envy of many, almost impregnable security of tenure. Where they have failed is in not gaining much control over the mechanisms for recruitment and training, both pre-service and in-service, the relevant qualifications, and promotion and general professional development.

It seems that the teacher bodies have, in the event, been more successful as 'unions' than 'associations'. The current plight of unemployed teachers, a consequence of over-training and the unexpected drop in pupil numbers, is illuminating. In 1978 the DES official figure was over 10,000, and the NUT figure, which included teachers who, after training, found other employment, was 24,000. Presumably the truth hovered somewhere in between, but in a society which had mourned over teacher shortages a decade earlier, it is a sorrowful figure. Sad as it is for anyone to be out of work, the ill-consequence for the consumer is heightened. During the 60s, with fierce pressure on colleges to produce many more teachers and with college totals reaching well over 100,000, there is little doubt that some sub-standard teachers were produced. The profession, not being in control of recruitment and eligibility, was not in a position to change the levers of supply and demand by, for instance, improving conditions of service in order to attract better quality recruits. Nowadays parents and pupils might protest that some unemployed teachers would be more suitable than some of those in employ. There is no adequate method for ensuring that the most competent teachers available are in the right jobs.

This seems to be an abiding characteristic of a nationalized monopoly like state education. It neither obeys the law of the market, nor is it planned efficiently. In a cut-throat commercial set-up, the poorer teachers would, according to the market theory, go to the wall and the better teachers rise. If the planning were objective and pure, the same end would result. The teachers would not accept this for obvious reasons: the unions would be acting contrary to their purpose if they did. Management, anxious to negotiate the administrative chores of education as peacefully as possible and already hamstrung by financial and other problems, is unlikely to add to its burdens by inventing an entirely new game of staff selection.

What is certain is that the teachers, however ill - defined their sociological position, are in a strong position in education's decision-making process, from Hamilton House down to the meekest classroom. Because of the perplexity of roles and objectives in the education service, management and labour, sometimes in agreement, sometimes not, provide the service and assess its performance, with billions annually spent within this charmed circle and with little of no independent evaluation about that expenditure. What actually happens in schools is clearly their prerogative to an enormous degree. The parents and pupils, at base, are no more lawfully acknowledged in the education process (unless schools and teachers choose so to operate) than patients in a hospital or passengers on a railway train.

The half-tones, social and professional, of teaching continue. It is a strange mix of unclarified strengths and weaknesses. Bradley Headstone today would probably feel just as much at home, and not at home, as when he said to Eugene Wrayburn, 'you think me of no more value than the dirt under your feet, and the casually caustic Wrayburn responded 'I assure you, Schoolmaster, I don't think about you.'

Essay subjects and seminar topics

1 It is objectively proposed that the education of the nation's children would benefit considerably if there were but 20% of the present teachers (about 100,000) but with higher training, much higher salaries, improved service conditions, and a complex pattern of technological equipment and sizeable ancillary staffs, all amounting to much the present outlay of resources. How should the teaching profession respond?

2 Devise a constitution and set of objectives for a General Teaching Council. How would such a body affect the day-by-day life of a school?

17 TEACHER-TRAINING

Candidates need to be able to read fluently and without unpleasant tones, write a fair hand, spell correctly, be well acquainted with the four rules of arithmetic and have some general acquaintance with history and geography.

'Regulations for admission, Borough Road College' (1846)

Intending students should note that it is the intention of the Secretary of State to introduce a general requirement that with effect from a given date...entrants to all undergraduate and postgraduate courses of initial training should be expected to have attained at least a Grade C in the G.C.E. 'O' level examination or a Grade 1 in the C.S.E. examination in both Mathematics and English. Alternatively they must satisfy the training institution concerned of numeracy and literacy to an equivalent level.

The Handbook of Degree and Advanced Courses (1979)

The history of the training of teachers runs parallel to the story of expanding state education and the rise of the teaching profession to its present strength, and it acts as a useful frame of reference for both narratives. The most important watershed was the very first one, when teacher-training became institutionalized. Once the collegiate mode was adopted, there was little structural and—in some commentators' view—not much more substantive change. *En masse* training in schools was followed by *en masse* teacher training, as opposed to a form of individual apprentice teaching, which gradually died away. The division of labour, so important in industry, applied everywhere, and the teacher doubling as clerk and registrar soon became as redundant as the barber-surgeon. Alongside this specialization there was a crop of law schools, theological schools and medical schools as, across the professional spectrum, training was institutionalized.

Just after the turn of the nineteenth century Joseph Lancaster opened a college at Borough Road, London, for and on behalf of the British and Foreign Society. This was England's first college, and, for practically the whole of the century, teacher-training, like teaching itself, was organized and controlled by the church, so much so that James Kay-Shuttleworth's attempt at forming a state college in the 1830s foundered on the sharp rocks of religious controversy. He did, along with E. C. Tuffnell, like himself a poor law official, manage to start the Battersea Normal School in 1840, but in 1841 the National Society countered with its own foundation, St Marks, Chelsea, which very soon took over the Battersea Institution. In a sudden spurt, there were 22 church colleges by 1845.

In 1846 Kay-Shuttleworth was instrumental in inaugurating the pupil-teacher system. This was a vestigial form of apprenticeship, from 13 to 18 with a stipend for the five-year period, and with the day split between 5½ hours teaching and 1½ hours learning. Prompted by the difficulties of formulating a state college system, this proved to be the last fling of that dying artifice, apprenticeship, and, from another angle, was an early and primitive form of secondary education.

Like just about all teacher-training, it was 'monitorial' in method; that is, the novitiates were shepherded and supervized by the mature and qualified members of the brethren. Aged 18, these pupil-teachers could compete for Queen's Scholarships for a training college course or, if unsuccessful, could stake some preferential claim for minor civil service posts. State monetary incentives were, as was characteristic of the era, used to tempt the colleges with, equally characteristic, the less entrancing prospect of inspection. The 200 pupil-teachers of the initial 1846 scheme became, by 1861, a legion of 14,000. By that year no fewer than 1,676 of the 2,065 in training were Queen's Scholars, bringing to the 35 colleges (all but seven of which were Church of England) £50,000 in state grants, out of an expenditure of £95,000.

Unluckily, the austere terms of the 1862 Revised Code ravaged teacher-training, and college numbers dropped immediately by 20%. The pupil-teacher system persisted, but much more use was made of localized pupil-teacher centres, like the Mount Pleasant Centre, opened in Liverpool in 1875. As the grants were reduced, so were the numbers of pupil-teachers, down to 9,000 by 1866, and teacher training remained in the doldrums until the end of the century.

In 1888 the Cross Commission on the Workings of the Elementary Education Acts suggested University Day Training Colleges, which, in practice, were non-residential degree-awarding departments. By 1901 there were 17 of these, while the colleges had slumped quite steeply. This gave a considerable impetus to university influence in teacher-training, and there gradually emerged the well-known three-year degree course, followed by a year's professional training for a postgraduate certificate in education. With the rise of secondary education after 1902 the pupil-teacher system flopped still more, from 11,000 in 1907 to 1,500 in 1913.

The accent was now entirely on college training, with the leas granted permission to build such agencies under the terms of the 1902 Act. Partly already overcommitted on novel secondary school enterprises and partly wary of building locally for national needs, the leas were slow to respond, until the temptation of a 75% grant proved irresistible and 22 colleges had been established by 1914.

By the 20s the pupil-teacher system had been commonly replaced by a routeway from elementary to secondary school, by scholarship, and then to college for two years, possibly with a brief 'student-teacher' posting beforehand. The heavily stuffed timetables of the era were not much different from those of 80 years before, and the concentration on mechanical drills had abated but little. I have had described to me by teachers qualifying before the First World War how, on school practice, the student was accompanied to and fro by a tutor, who kept watch the entire time, a method known to footballers as man-for-man marking. In short, this was the pupil-teacher system institutionalized—the careful division of training into strict academic and professional confines, each marked by a detailed and personal oversight, meant that pupil-teacherhood had merely been collectivized.

The universities continued to be prominent, and, after the 1944 McNair Report on the supply and training of teachers, universities established departments of education around which local colleges clustered like chicks round the mother hen, and the Area Training Organizations were set up as what McNair termed 'an organic federation of approved training institutions'. The influential Robbins Report (1963) proposed that the training colleges should be re-named Colleges of Education, and that the universities should, administratively, absorb them, a suggestion made earlier by half the McNair Committee. The names were changed, but the leas very much the representatives of the employers, were, at the time of McNair, anxious to cling hold of managerial control. What in fact happened in practice from the 1920s onward was that the universities had oversight of the academic and the leas (except for the church colleges) had supervision of the administrative element of the colleges, with increasingly large financial support from the central government.

The impact of Robbins and the addition, in 1963, of a third year to teacher-training created a boom in the colleges, peaking well above 100,000 places and as late as 1970 projecting a need for 130,000 places in teacher-training. There was the move to an all-graduate profession, especially after the James Report on *Teacher Education and Training* (1972), with the Bachelor of Education degree becoming a standard qualification. At the peak there were something like 160 colleges in being.

Unfortunately, almost at the moment this pinnacle was being achieved, the fabric was crumbling under the sapping blows of reduced birth-rates which surprised and dismayed the estimates. The call for rationalization was sounded, in part because of a belief that collegiate units should be larger and diversified in function. Size became important. The earliest colleges had been, on average, no more than 60 strong. It had been the fashion to sit around the principal in an evening, the students primly embroidering while their mentor read to them improving literature. Slowly, the numbers had grown, until, by the 70s, colleges less than 1000 strong might be suspect, and all were requested to think in terms of providing courses other than just for teachers. The *volte face* was dramatic. Between 1973 and 1975 there was a contraction of student numbers to 61,000 places and a reduction, chiefly by merger, of the number of colleges. A second phase occurred from then until 1977, resulting in a reduction to 47,000 places and the closure and amalgamation of more colleges. A target of 45,000 places, minimally, has been set.

It was a traumatic spasm in the history of teacher education. There was a seemingly endless round of wheeler-dealing, followed closely by as inexhaustible a cycle of recrimination. There were mergers with polytechnics and mergers with universities, and at the moment about 80 colleges apart from the university departments of education have emerged, bloody but unbowed, from the carnage. These are known as Institutes or Colleges of Education; a few Colleges of Education remain; and there are also a group of Polytechnic Departments of Education. The upshot was that, in the summer of 1978, some 16,000 teachers took up their first appointment. They amounted to about half of what the statisticians refer to as 'successful exits'. They numbered some 33,000 of whom 18,200 were graduates, including B.Eds, and 14,800 were 'others', including graduate equivalents.

Thus, inexorably, teacher-education reflects the mainstream of educational history. First, the numbers rose and fell with the tidal changes in the pupil population, and, second, the tendency of educational and other institutions to become bigger seems also to have been followed, as colleges have gradually grown, rationalized, and merged, just as comprehensive schools have in the schools sector. The 60 students of the 1870s became the 1000 and more of the 1970s, and what needs to be explored is the extent to which, this is part of a general, Weber-like 'rationalization' in most aspects of life, with, for instance, the gradual swing from the many small retail outlets—the corner shop of the romantic urban idyll—to the supermarket and the department store. When in chapter 26, the notion of the school or college as an institution is exampled, the point will be raised again.

The basic tenets of teacher-training have not dramatically altered during these vicissitudes. The apprenticeship style of pupil-training was institutionalized, and that was that. The pupil-teacher dualism of personal and professional instruction was adopted by the colleges, where, in many, the distinction between the 'academic' and the 'educational' work of the student was jealously preserved, despite the strictures of avant-garde tutors that a coherent, rounded approach might be more effective. The James Report *Teacher Education and Training*, 1972, beatified this dualistic approach, and diversification (despite the advantage of mixing up potential teachers with others) underpins the division between academic and professional training sharply and sometimes in an end-on way. The university fourth 'certificate' year has ever been open to that criticism of making professional training a postscript to rather than an integral part of the student's education.

It is possible that the inclination of teacher-training toward this approach, with the universities increasingly offering pre-service and in-service diplomas, certificates and degrees, has too consciously sustained the age-old academic pedigree of the teacher. That is not an anti-intellectual point: it is a reasoned recognition that the role of the teacher in society is by no means limited to scholarship, and that the pursuit or grasp of knowledge, as presently defined by its scholarly arbiters, may not automatically be related to children's needs in modern, urban society. It may be that it has never been so, and that much that has been trafficked in schools, as a kind of bastardized assortment of higher learning, has frequently been inadequate in terms of the skills and information children required. This, to the extent it is true, has arisen from a view of education as an academic system and not a social service. This is not because scholarship of itself is wrong; far from it. What is wrong is the idea that it is suitable for dilution for everyone: education and scholarship are not identical.

The opposite is just as troublesome, in its overplaying of the pragmatic. What has always been alarming has been the antipathy expressed by many teachers about their own training, usually along the lines of the education theory being too idealistic and the academic work too remote. The 'practical' version suggested by some teachers takes us back to the 'union/profession' controversy discussed in chapter 11, for it appears that some favour the 'sitting with Fred' method, with the student-teacher merely learning a trade, entirely on the job. They posit this against the purportedly over-theoretical, unduly academic offerings of the colleges and universities. But practice without a sound conceptual frame is dangerous. The technically efficient teacher with no sense of philosophic objectives is as frightening as the lunatic armed with a loaded shot-gun in a crowded store.

At the time of the English Civil War Sir John Fairfax, the parliamentary general, said that all the scribes and pharisees were on one side and all the publicans and sinners on the other. In the practice-theory squabble, neither the pseudo-realists nor the neo-idealists seem to have the proper and most efficacious balance.

Essay subjects and seminar topics

1 Is teaching a trade, like brick-laying, with a set of skills to be mastered, or a vocation, like the church, with a personal conviction and commitment a prerequisite? Whether it is either or a compound of the two, how best might recruitment and training be organized?

2 Teachers are often virulently critical of the weaknesses of their own training, and yet, when threatened by outsiders seeking to exert influence, they defend themselves stoutly on the grounds that they are the trained and qualified experts. Discuss both postulates, and consider whether they are compatible.

18 TEACHING IN THE FUTURE

A mother was trying to make her son get up and go to school. He was very obstinate. 'Give me two reasons' she argued, 'why you shouldn't get up and go to school.' 'Well,' her stubborn son replied, 'for one think the kids don't like me, and, for another, I don't like the kids'. The mother paused a moment, and then she countered. 'Alright, shall I give you two reasons why you should get up and go to school?' 'Carry on', said the son. 'Firstly,' said the mother, 'you're forty-three years old, and, secondly, you're the headteacher.'

It has been estimated that the teacher makes 200,000 inter-personal contacts a year, and if, like the teacher in the story, they are fruitless ones, then considerable damage and waste is the sad consequence. The professional-lay relationship promoted by the teacher is of the essence, and this becomes particularly true if the lesson of chapter 8 (about the effect of home background on the child's educational attainment) and the argument of chapter 12 (about the need to regard pupils as consumers, not products) are accepted. A 'service' rather than a 'producer' role and a role adjusted to adult as well as child requirements is very different to the traditional task of the teacher, as didactic transmitter of narrowly defined pieces of information.

It may be helpful to see the issue in breadth, by relating it to the dozens of other professional-lay relationships of which daily life sometimes seems to consist. There are a wide range of public professionals who are now locked in what must sometimes seem like mortal combat with the laity. It is a lengthy list, for it includes not only doctors, child psychologists, other medical workers, social workers and teachers, but prison and probation workers, policemen, public health officials, social security and supplementary benefits officers, housing managers and a dozen more. Given that the state recognizes a public obligation to right the chief social ills of poverty, ill-health, ignorance, disorder and homelessness, these are all the agents of such interventionist policies, and as such they are placed in as extensive a series of professional-lay relationships.

In popular folk-lore these are not always engaging figures—the authoritarian teacher, the disciplinarian nurse, the over-clinical doctor, the condescending social worker, the abrasive social security officer, and so on. However tiny the sparks of fire which give rise to such billowing clouds of smoke, they are still part of the nation's gut reaction to public servants. Yet, in the hurly-burly of domestic activity they are scarcely distinguishable from ordinary humanity. They stop short of consuming their young; and they cultivate their gardens with conventional English assiduity. For many years one has despaired of teachers who teach Tennyson by day and watch Kojak by night. If I may quote an extract from an article of mine on this theme (*Teachers' World*, 13 February 1974):

One explanation is in itself a cultural one. There is a cultural image of the teacher in our society, and it portrays the teacher as the purveyor of rather highbrow and somewhat antiquated cults. Some commentators even go so far as to say that the teacher's obsession with 'reading' is an example of this, given that we are moving into so substantially an audio-visual era. But more overt illustrations lie in the musical, moral, religious, literary and fashion fields. For, in turn, the teacher under heavy pressure from society, feels obliged, perhaps forced, to accept these as part of his or her teaching persona.

Imagine, then, the young teacher, affectionate adherent of the new musical sounds, blissfully happy in a well-adjusted pre-marital sexual relationship, agnostic, currently reading Couples *and* Portnoy's Complaint *and with rather an extravagant yen for jewellery. She may well find herself during a normal day's teaching, attempting to promote the appreciation of some classical musical item, defending the sanctity of marriage, attending a religious assembly, getting cross about the girls reading risqué illustrated stories and disciplining them for disobeying some over-zealous rule about skirt or hair lengths.*

It is this refusal to be human and this fear of being human, of being one's true self, in the professional pale which helps sustain the gap between the professionals and clients beset by difficulties and thus at their most vulnerable and human. The young, the sick, the poor, the homeless, all these groups of social casualties, find themselves faced by complicated and incomprehensible procedures negotiated by varying species of techno-bureaucrat.

Along with and as part of that process of the, in Max Weber's word, 'rationalization' of our agencies has gone the parallel evolution of a restricting professionalization. What the Webbs called the 'prescribed qualification' grew to be the norm for every specific role in the providing of services, on the respectable ground that the user should be properly protected from inefficiency. But all the professions have slavishly adhered to the historic fate mapped out for professions. They have become bureaucratized, defensive about manning and function, haunted by false fears of 'dilution', jittery about evaluation and open accountability, jargon-plagued, status-conscious, and sheltering, in a pother of insecurity, behind a barricade of mystiques.

Now this sober caricature of the tight-lipped, tight-minded professional operating in secluded institutional gloom would not matter quite so much were it not that many individual practitioners are advocating and piloting exactly the opposite type of method. Particularly where mothers and small children foregather, there is talk of moves being made towards lay involvement and assistance in these services, of less institutionalized approaches, of more informal and open-ended treatments and so forth. Some (not all) aspects of the playgroup movement illustrate this tendency toward enlightened and sponsored self-help, toward a genuine partnership of professionals and lay persons in the provision of a service.

Now it is increasingly apparent that one cannot educate, and otherwise treat children, in isolation. In education it becomes clearer that those few hours a day in school are of relatively small consequence when set against the influence of the environment at large and particularly the home. Medicine is a little better than education in this regard: doctors would scoff at performing the kind of tasks which teachers feel would place in hazard their professional prestige. They do not, for instance, circle our towns slowly, spooning medicaments into patients three times a day: teachers have yet to delegate that category of assignment to ancillaries, let alone lay people, and, their case-hardened politicoes might note, doctors still retain high professional status despite having abandoned total supervision of treatment.

Whichever subject we turn to—child welfare, health, education, law and order—we find it has produced, in society, an all-permeating layer or dimension. There is a health dimension, an educative dimension, and so on, with each, of course, interlocked with the other. So powerful is this that no professional should ignore it, and proceed to practise, so to speak, behind closed doors in a socio-economic vacuum. My guess is that the Victorians rightly perceived that the 'preventive principle' was the valid one, but wrongly chose the policy of institutionalism, of incarceration, of putting their social ills in quarantine, to implement that principle. Their refusal to see social difficulties in an across-the-board and generalist manner and, subsequently, their refusal to come to terms with the public at large meant an aggravation of those ills. By not mobilizing the community sufficiently to understand and tackle the problems, they were soon forced, in the most part, to replace prevention with prescription, by restricting most of the necessary knowledge and techniques to the professionals. Sheltered within the institutions, they ensured that the problems would never enjoy the opportunity of general eradication and, as we have seen, the professionals, and their institutions, have multiplied and prospered.

The specialists may have to 're-professionalize' themselves, or, put negatively, they may have to demythologize their professionalism. This they might do by an interlock of two features. One is the willingness to share their mysteries with the laity, and the other is the setting of the activity within the clientele's cultural focus. An important consequence of this is that, in style and format, it becomes open-ended.

It offers no doctrinaire solution. It begins with the notion that, in concert, parents and young children have needs, in health, welfare and education terms, which are couched in the elements of the strengths and weaknesses of their surrounds—and that the answer must, organically, become an integral, living part of that environmental tissue if it is to survive. By refusing firstly to see parents and youngsters interdependently, by refusing secondly to see health and education and other social factors interdependently, and by refusing thirdly to approach the question with a predetermined response, the professional-lay relationship is turned on its head.

That is no exaggeration. This projection of the concept of the professional as the facilitator and energizer is a topsy-turvy one. It is about the professional being a social explorer rather than a social defender, and about being an adult educator as well as a child educator. It is, perhaps as important as anything, about a change in style, with the teachers of the future the convenors and the barkers for custom of their crafts in the community. The conservationist tendencies of all professions, including teaching, are very pronounced. Training, background, inclination, temperament: these and other facets help to perpetuate the traditional approach, and to reverse it would require radical changes in recruitment, training, personnel and resource deployment and in many other fields.

There is no point in those who favour the argument being over optimistic, nor in those who dislike the idea being unduly alarmed. It would be misleading to blur the issue and pretend it would be a simple change. Consider, for instance, the actual chalk-face question of what flexibility might mean, daily, in the classroom, were service-oriented teaching to be introduced.

The head of mathematics in a large comprehensive may decide to adopt a traditional syllabus, and set by ability. In the same school one may find another departmental head—in English, perhaps—who deploys randomly arrived at mixed-ability groups, and an *avant garde* approach. Both may cluck as anxiously as any mother hen over his or her charges as individuals, but, for each individual, the basic choice has already occurred.

In a primary school one could take the reading scheme as an example. In many schools—not all—a particular reading programme will be adopted, and that will be that. However diligently the teachers may, given that decision, assist each individual, it is unlikely to compare with the zealousness with which they insist that the selected mode is the superior one.

This does not arise from an authoritarian stance, but from a well-intentioned flimflam liberalistic viewpoint, encapsulated by two head teachers' quotes: 'I wouldn't tell my teachers what or how to teach: they must be free to choose' and 'the teachers here find that (brand name) reading-scheme works best for them'.

This very open-endedness about treatments is the core of the argument. If teachers, either in staff and department groups or individually, disagree, respectably and validly, over methods and content, then these blanket applications of approaches must be suspect.

As long as several reading approaches are professionally acceptable, it can scarcely be entertained that the 30 infants starting at school A are all automatically best suited to ita, whereas, at school B, a couple of streets away, an intake of 30 there will all merrily benefit to the full from the exploits of Janet and John. Certainly, some of the most successful teachers of reading assemble a mart of possibilities and, often in consultation with parents and with the aid of some simple testing, ascertain which is the preferable approach.

The same applies to the sterile argument about 'informal' versus 'formal'. Surely the rational conclusion to be drawn from the present state of the debate is that either is likely to suit some children some of the time—and often the same children for different subjects.

Similarly with teacher attitudes. One should be as suspicious of the Simon Legree figure—the unwaveringly harsh disciplinarian—as of the Aunt Pollyanna figure—the unremittingly syrupy softheart. Stick or carrot all the time for all children?

This can then be projected from teacher to school. Many people must be horrified that some schools feel obliged to adopt a 'mould', and that the question of 'parental choice' is cast in this manner. Do you want a 'traditional' or a 'progressive' school, or a half-baked school with some traditional and some progressive subjects? Often without prior consultation or testing, would you be willing, as a parent, to plunge a child into such a 'mould'?

The inflexibility is unrelenting. Be it a neo-Tyndale or a pseudo-Manchester Grammar School caricature, the rigidity of the process must be wrong for some children all of the time, and all of the children some of the time. Deliberately, the case is strongly urged for the substitution of the secluded, private agent by the outgoing public activist. It is because teachers who qualify in 1984 will, assuming a lowering of the retirement age to 60, retire in 2022, and the last infants taught by such a dedicated teacher might expect to sight the dawn of the twenty-second century.

If teachers are to shrug off their Victorian mantle and look keenly to this future, then such changes of attitude will be imperative.

Essay subjects and seminar topics

1 In Shaw's *The Doctor's Dilemma*, Sir Walpole Cutler's sole treatment was to remove the nuciform sac on the grounds that everyone suffers from blood-poisoning. How fair is it to suggest that many teachers have a similar obsession with a given approach or method, justifying it on the grounds that it works best for them?

2 A standard response of teachers, asked to involve parents in the education of their (the parents') children is that they 'don't like having people in the classroom with them', as if children were somehow a distinct species. Are teachers ultra-sensitive about privacy and seclusion from the adult world; if so, why, does it matter, and, assuming it does, what can be done about it?

3 EDUCATION AND THE SCHOOL

PRIMARY SCHOOLS

19 THE PRIMARY SCHOOL AND ITS STRUCTURE

I have come here just in time to save a noble institution from ruin. There is more danger to the plan from misguided committees and weak schoolmasters...than there is, or ever was, from pecuniary circumstances and I am convinced that if I had not travelled into these parts the plan would have had a death-blow here. Here is a noble school-room, which cost £1,700 building, capable of holding 600 to 700 boys; a liberal-minded set of men are the committee, but all Taffys or Welchmen... The school was three days ago a scene of disorder and riot, now a pin may be heard to drop, and order is the order of the day.

Joseph Lancaster, letter to his daughter
regarding the Welsh Charity School in Liverpool (1809)

When, the morning after her marriage, Queen Victoria, according to *The Times*, was strolling at dawn with Prince Albert, Lord Palmerston grumbled 'that's no way to go about getting a Prince of Wales'. His anxiety was misplaced. Queen Victoria's nine children helped swell the population explosion, and, although their education was more exclusive if no more lenient than that of their common fellows, the necessity to educate was strongly believed from palace to cottage.

The story of the primary school is essentially the gradual gelling of this belief (for whatever reasons it was held) with the problem of numbers. Historically, the decisions and chance happenings which led to the institutionalization of all young children for educational purposes, as opposed to most of them remaining at home with but a few 'institutionalized', was the chief watershed. There were, apart from those for rich families, some schools; indeed, in 1818, 17% of England's 18,000 schools were dames' schools. Some were the rosy, cosy little nooks of well-scrubbed infants and comfortable matron of the 'Water Babies' picture, but those in the big cities were often squalid. Liverpool's first medical officer of health, Dr Duncan, reported several in that city's cellars. Forty or 50 squalling children, their parents grafting away long hours at uncongenial labour, in a cellar no more than 12 yards square; that was the norm, with, on one or another occasion, the dame dying of cholera in the corner.

Then there were the Proprietary schools, founded, like the best business enterprises of the time, as joint stock companies, and there were hundreds of often maladministered Endowed Schools. There were the many Charity schools, and, alongside these, the Schools of Industry, to instruct youngsters in a trade, and there was also hundreds of Sunday Schools.

By the 1820s, the voluntary movement was well under way, mainly under the auspices of the British and Foreign, and the National Societies, so that England's thousands of schools (in numbers not that much less than now) presented a weird and bizarre collection of usually tiny schools; the average had no more than 50 pupils.

It was a time of transition, not only in terms of increased population, but in the movements towards an urban and industrialized existence. Just as the early ramshackle workshops and foundries represented a mid-way stage between the domestic and the factory system of industry, so did this *ad hoc* collation of schools act as a corresponding bridge between little or no education outside home or apprenticeship and the dogma of the large school. Teaching itself was normally on the tutorial plan, with work prepared (hence 'prep') for hearing by the teacher either singly or in a small covey of pupils, so that differential teaching contact was often the approach. Other social difficulties were treated as ignorance was. Poverty was met by the Old Poor Law system of each parish caring for its own paupers in small poorhouses or through outdoor relief. Disease was met by quarantine, home treatment or, occasionally, by hospitals, with random bunches of the sick haphazardly housed. Crime was met by the 'watch and ward' or 'know everyone' system, with watchmen and others serving on a very localized basis and criminals gaoled in district bridewells or sometimes in county gaols.

But as efficient management and the division of labour was lauded by the apostles of free trade and as the 'mass' nature of ignorance, poverty, disease and crime fluttered more middle- and upper-class dove-cotes, there were dramatic changes in these social services. This was the age when, in answer to 'mass' urban and rural poverty, parishes were amalgamated into 'unions' and huge, gaunt workhouses were erected; when, in answer to ':mass' disease, like cholera or typhus, the large general hospitals were built; when, in answer to 'mass' crime and disorder, in the towns especially, the great prisons, like Pentonville or Walton, were constructed; and when, in answer to 'mass' ignorance, sizeable schools were established.

The Victorians turned to the 'factory formula' for social succour, because it seemed to serve them so beneficially in educational terms. This is no idle speculation. The Victorians had the advantage over us Elizabethans of knowing why schools were established in that image. 'The principle in schools and manufactories is the same', they argued, while Sir Thomas Barnard, earnest advocate of the large, new schools, said that 'their grand principle (was) the division of labour applied to intellectual purposes'. Samuel Taylor Coleridge spoke of the school as 'a vast moral steam engine' and Andrew Bell, writing of 'this intellectual and moral engine' said of the school that 'like the steam engine or spinning machinery, it diminishes labour and multiplies work'.

Others were urging similar views in the other social fields, and the school, like the hospital, the prison and the workhouse, followed the factory in architectural detail. This was quite overt. The original Victorian schools were, like the original factories and mills, barnlike, single-storey and cavernous places, with one eagle eye, headteacher or mill-owner, able to comprehend all. As the division of labour grew more sophisticated, physically separate workshops were introduced, and, particularly in the School Board era, schools followed suit. Under the influence of the London School Board architect, Mr E. R. Robson, the German notion was introduced of, instead of the vast hall with tiered seating and galleries, the central hall with classrooms abutting. What might be called 'economic streaming' (the replacement of the all-round craftsman by the production line and the division of labour by specific function) was aped by schools as they streamed ever more rigorously by what came to be called 'age, aptitude and ability'. Workhouses were most firmly streamed by category of pauper, including the infamous separation of married couples, while hospitals became much more alive to the classification of patients by sex and illness. Prisons, so long haphazard mixes of ne'er do wells, began to allocate to wings according to offence.

The employment or professional structure fell inexorably into line. As these social 'factories' became separated in this manner, the new managerial style was borrowed from the mill or foundry, with its works manager at centre, and its foremen or overlookers in charge of the different workshops. Thus the workhouse master, the hospital matron, the prison governor and the headteacher found themselves supervizing the overseer in the dormitory, the sister in the ward, the warder in the wing and the teacher in the classroom, respectively. The Victorians, their noting the success of incarcerating their work-force within factory walls, decided to do likewise for the four 'P's of nineteenth-century social ills: the pauper, the patient, the prisoner and the pupil.

The 'factory formula' was thus applied, deliberately and consciously, across the board, and the teacher who believes that the school, as we have inherited it, was begotten of undefiled educational ideals would be misled. Population, urbanism and the factory resulted (as chapter 1 described) in 'congregation'; this, in turn, created a new slant on old problems, with social troubles in 'congregation' form. The answer, was in short, 'congregation'. The four 'P's were pressed and crowded together into institutions built on factory lines.

The most typical and all-pervading version of this development was the Monitorial System, with whom the names of Joseph Lancaster (of the British and Foreign Society) and Andrew Bell (of the National Society: he hit upon the monitorial scheme in Madras) are usually linked. In this pyramidal system, the teacher taught the monitors and the monitors taught the children. A thousand and more could, it was claimed, be taught by one teacher, and Bell saw it as an advance on the steam engine, 'for', he wrote, 'unlike the mechanical powers, this intellectual and moral engine, the more work it has to perform the greater is the facility and expendition with which it is performed, and the greater the degree of perfection to which it is carried.'

Although the Bell and Lancaster methods differed in details (the former had a complex pattern of brainy/slow-witted duos and a veritable hierarchy of ushers, while the latter stuck simply to one monitor for 20 children) what they, and other monitorial protagonists accomplished, was that all children were being taught at once and in huge numbers. There was, overnight, a change from the smallish school, with frequently a tutorial approach, to the largish school, with classes taught simultaneously with dictation, reading round the class and similar features. There has really been no fundamental change of strategy in elementary-cum-primary schooling since. The grand change from a basically private, chiefly religious set of schools, subsidized by the state, to a basically public network of schools, with some retaining religious affiliations has been alluded to (chapter 10) but it did not affect the internal structure of the schools as much.

There is both a physical and a psychological conservationism about these matters. Once a school is built, it usually stays put for many years, and its architecture dictates how the school will be organized. If classrooms are constructed to hold 30 or so children, then there is little else one can do with them. Once the image of the school was accepted as being of the hall and classroom type, it became increasingly difficult to shake men's minds into conceiving otherwise of the school. There is a reluctance in some quarters to tolerate even the slight modification of the open-plan school, which, oddly, is in some senses a return to the cavernous expanse of the early nineteenth-century school. The number of primary schools with pre-1903 accommodation is 8,300 out of a total of 23,300 — 36% — and that kind of architectural determinism is difficult to withstand.

In terms of external administration and funding the same buildings have obviously undergone several changes of notice-board and other appellations. My own elementary education took place in one example. It had been, when my grandfather attended, a British Society school known as the township school. It was rebuilt as the very last School Board school to be so sanctioned in England and Wales, but, by the time my mother, father and both my in-laws arrived there it was a 'provided' or 'council' school, and so it remained for my brother's and my own (and my brother- and sister-in-law's) early schooling. By the time my wife was in attendance, it had become, under the terms of the 1944 Act, a county primary or maintained school. Throughout these managerial changes it never faltered in its internal organization, nor could it have, given its six classrooms off a central hall. It still stands today, and there are hundreds like it, many of them with longer histories.

So the primary schools of today, in physical structure and, by that token, organizational method, have descended from the Victorian age, and we have inherited a format quite consciously styled on the factory, with, it should be added, a flavour of the barracks. For the Victorians also recognized that the military machine had had its successes, and, although that trait is more noticeable in hospital, police, workhouse and prison supervision, schools, not least architecturally, were not free from it.

The most extreme version of the Victorian mode of rational cost-accounting in all matters was that stated by the Utilitarians, the followers of Jeremy Bentham, who believed that the sum of each individual's pursuit of self-interest led, in aggregate, to the greatest happiness for the greatest number. In education, they invented the Chrestomathic School, that is, the 'useful learning'school. Utility was the yardstick for its organization and business efficiency was the criterion of its curriculum. The famous Hazelwood school, not far from Birmingham, was the supreme illustration, and it serves to demonstrate how profoundly the Utilitarian cause was pressed. There were 43 rules, like the 'place-capturing' principle, or the 'comparative proficiency' principle. The idea of competitiveness and 'positions' in class stemmed from such experiments. The actual physical location of brighter and dimmer pupils in different parts of the class, with the ultimate of the 'top of the form' in the place of honour, is still to be found, in moderated fashion,in some of our primary schools. The school bell at Hazelwood clanged its sonorous cues no less than 250 times each week, beginning at six in the morning and signalling the onset and end to every activity, however minute, throughout the day until bed-time. The bell, like the factory hooter, guided the inmates of the school along a carefully prescribed routeway, and the pupils, like many a mill-hand, were on piecework. They received marks for good work and forfeited them, in fines, for bad work, with a boy banker, on 1% commission, to keep and tally the accounts. A final sanction, should fines prove futile for the more obdurate pupils, was solitary confinement in a small, dark chamber.

The Chrestomathic School was the classic transfer of industrial and commercial practice to education and it now appears little more than a rather unpleasant absurdity. Nonetheless, the cost-accountancy of ticks and crosses and the competition for places still continues in many schools, and, where this has lapsed, it is arguable that the various systems of silver and golden stars and other awards are but a milder modification. Certainly the tradition of physical punishment so prevalent over the years in British schools as opposed to its much lighter usage and eventual abolition in most other western countries, was preserved in the monitorial system. When Joseph Lancaster created order out of chaos in the Liverpool Welsh School, he may well have indulged some of his favourite devices. Over against improving pictures for prizes, he would, by way of chastisement, shackle legs, tie hands to a log behind the back, bind pupils for detention and even place them in a basket on the school-roof. There is no truth in the legend that his prize pupil was Houdini.

Essay subjects and seminar topics

1 A varied approach is now sometimes demanded by educationists, with some teachers teaching small groups, while, with audio-visual aids, another teacher might oversee a much larger group, or some children might pursue their studies privately, and so on. Assume an Edwardian ten-classroom/central-hall school, with 100 each of infants, early juniors and later juniors, and eleven teachers. Work out a flexible as opposed to a class-based space-time table for that establishment.

2 Some forms of group work or joint parent-child projects are based on cooperation as opposed to competition. How pronounced is this in schools, and how distinct a philosophic change does it represent? Lady Plowden once wryly spoke of children, encouraged in collaboration in primary schools, being accused of cheating in their secondary schools!

20 PRIMARY SCHOOLS: CONTENT

The education of Mr Polly did not follow this picture very closely. He went for some time to a National School, which was run on severely economical lines to keep down the rates, by a largely untrained staff; he was set sums to do that he did not understand, and that no one made him understand; he was made to read the Catechism and Bible with the utmost industry and an entire disregard of punctuation or significance; caused to imitate writing copies and drawing copies; given object lessons upon sealing-wax and silk-worms and potato bugs and ginger and iron and suchlike things; taught various other subjects his mind refused to entertain; and afterwards, when he was about twelve, he was jerked by his parents to 'finish off' in a private school of dingy aspect and still dingier pretensions, where there were no object lessons, and the studies of book-keeping and French were pursued (but never effectually overtaken) under the guidance of an elderly gentleman, who wore a nondescript gown and took snuff, wrote copperplate, explained nothing, and used a cane with remarkable dexterity and gusto.

Mr Polly went into the National School at six, and he left the private school at fourteen, and by that time his mind was in much the same state that you would be in, dear reader, if you were operated upon for appendicitis by a well-meaning, boldly enterpising, but rather overworked and underpaid butcher boy, who was superseded towards the climax of the operation by a left-handed clerk of high principles but intemperate habits — that is to say, it was in a thorough mess. The nice little curiosities and willingness of a child were in a jumbled and thwarted condition, hacked and cut about — the operators had left, so to speak, all their sponges and ligatures in the mangled confusion — and Mr Polly had lost much of his natural confidence so far as figures and sciences and languages and the possibilities of learning things were concerned. He thought of the present world no longer as a wonderland of experiences, but as a geography and history, as the repeating of names that were hard to pronounce, and the lists of products and populations and heights and lengths, and as lists and dates — oh! and Boredom indescribable. He thought of religion as the recital of more or less incomprehensible words that were hard to remember, and of the Divinity as of a limitless Being having the nature of a schoolmaster and making infinite rules, known and unknown, rules that were always ruthlessly enforced, and with an infinite capacity for punishment, and, most horrible of all to think of, limitless powers of espial. (So to the best of his ability he did not think of that unrelenting eye.) He was uncertain about the spelling and pronunciation of most of the words in our beautiful but abundant and perlexing tongue — that especially was a pity, because words attracted him, and under happier conditions he might have used them well — he was always doubtful whether it was eight sevens or nine eights that was sixty-three (he knew no method for settling the difficulty), and he thought the merit of a drawing consisted in the care with which it was 'lined in'. 'Lining in' bored him beyond measure.

H. G. Wells *The History of Mr Polly* (1910)

Although the curriculum of the primary school has been subject to more variety than its internal structure, the conservation of content and approach has perhaps remained uppermost. The School Board period was a seminal one for what are now primary schools. The mechanical attainments of the three 'R's and the 'catechetical instruction' of the Charity and the Monitorial Schools had been inherited, and these, together with other subjects accepted in the later Victorian school, remain, in substance, the fodder of today's school. The daily dosage of reading, the daily exercise in maths (normally at the beginning of the day, avowedly while children are 'fresh'; as if literature is more suitable than mathematics for the 'stale' child!) the periodized time-table, the rituals of registration, of rote-learning, of 'doing lines' and 'staying in'—all became recognizable elements of the elementary-cum-primary set-up. The Revised Code of 1862 also introduced the notion of 'Standard I'. 'Standard II' and so on.

A school of 120 at that time might have a teacher and two pupil-teachers, probably no more than 14 years old. A typical reading card for infants read: 'sit on a sod and nod to me. A cat sits on a sod and nods to a lad. A lad sits on a sod and nods to a cat and to me. It is not a sin to sit on a sod. Am I to sit on a sod and nod? No.'

The picture of lad and cat nodding affectionately (and without sin) to one another across the sod is silly enough, but one might pause a moment to compare it with the inanities of many modern infant readers, which celebrate the suburban exploits of those impeccable quartets, mummy, daddy, son and daughter, with the ineluctable Rover barking tirelessly in the background. It is perhaps the unrelatedness of the material to the ordinary realities of life which makes for the similarity, together with remarkable staying power of subjects, once entered on the timetable. The regulations for most Board Schools, followed a schedule of 'essential' subjects (religious education, reading, writing, arithmetic, grammar and composition, history and geography, vocal music, drill, needlework) and 'discretionary' subjects (book-keeping, drawing, elementary science). Although the labels have altered somewhat, this pattern is not much removed from that of modern times. It might be claimed that such a list, interpreted widely, exhausts the possibilities and that it represents much of what every child, in whatever epoch, requires for his early education. The point is that the radical overhaul of primary curriculum has not perhaps been as dramatic as some—both exponents and opponents—might claim.

Rote-learning and other forms of memorization persist, especially of hymns, tables and poems. The maintenance of religious education, by law, is a minor piece of conservancy in itself. The initial impetus of organized religion as the ambit for elementary education has proved powerful, both in retention of church schools and in the fact that religious education is the only compulsory school subject.

By dint of 'standards' in the Revised Codes, School Board regulations, a succession of other fiats, the cyclic nature of training and the consensus of view of teachers themselves, 'academic freedom' has been part-myth and part-shibboleth. Schools are amazingly uniform in terms of the skills and information they are attempting to transmit.

Nor have attitudes changed unduly, in a purely educational sense, from when Dotheboys Hall was, in Dickens' phrase, an 'incipient Hell'. At the time of the Abdication of Edward VIII in 1936, the headmaster of my local council school paraded his charges, four abreast, in a huge circle. As they wound around him, he extracted any children walking twine-toed and caned them, for he believed Mrs Simpson to be so afflicted and theorized that herein lay some devil's mark. Several children were caned more than once. Ever adaptable, the children soon realized it was safer to walk splay-footed until, in my brother's words (he was present: readers will be relieved to note that, owing to extreme youth, I was not) the procession resembled 'a mass imitation of Charlie Chaplin!'

Although few teachers reached, one would hope, such levels of harsh eccentricity, that kind of approach was not unusual. A dead hand seemed to grasp schooling of infants and juniors, certainly until after the Second World War. The child in an 1875-classroom would probably have felt equally uncomfortable or comfortable, as his temperament and aptitude suggested, in a 1935 classroom.

One major reason for this was the survival, with minor qualifications, of a particular view of how the learning process occurs. John Locke, the seventeenth-century philosopher, had propounded the idea of the *tabula rasa*, the blank pad of the child's mind, awaiting whatever marks the teacher or experience might wish to inscribe. 'The difference so observable', wrote Locke, 'in men's understanding and parts does not arise so much from their natural faculties as acquired habits. He would be laughed at that should go about to make a fine dancer out of a country hedger at past fifty.' The Lockean view that 'practice must settle the habit of doing, without reflecting on the rule' was elaborated by the Benthamites as they applied to education their normal yardstick of 'utility'. What was required were those 'facts' which could be deemed useful, and they could be inserted into the mental container of the child at will. The child was father to the man; a mini-adult, to be treated as a 'little man', and dressed, as Victorian portraits denote, accordingly.

What came to be known vulgarly as 'mug and jug' psychology, is brilliantly illustrated in the first chapter of two Victorian books. In the opening pages of *Hard Times* (1854) Dickens burlesqued the contemporary obsession with 'facts' in the characters of Mr Gradgrind and Mr Bounderby and the teacher, Mr M'choakumchild. In the opening chapter of John Stuart Mill's *Autobiography* (begun in 1853-54) fiction indeed became fact. His father, James Mill, was the arch-proponent of mug-juggery and the Benthamites' leading educationist. He subjected his own son to a merciless and alarming regimen. Mill mastered English about the same time he mastered walking, and, at three, had moved on to Greek. By seven he had read the main Greek and English histories, and begun his studies of Latin, algebra, chemistry, philosophy and economics. He finished up with a 'mental crisis'—what now would probably be termed a nervous breakdown—and, according to some retrospective calculations, an IQ of 265!

The Utilitarian heritage is a strong one. The cult of pseudo-realism in many staff rooms testifies to this, with its firm beliefs in 'getting some facts into them' and its profound faith in the systematic drilling of children in procedures and pieces of knowledge. Recent surveys indicate what most observers had already guessed: that the opposing view of the learning process has not had so pronounced an affect on English primary schools as had been thought. Although, since 1945, a considerable body of knowledge and sentiment had opted for a less mechanistic approach—the so-called progressive method—it is now apparent that this has not been all that influential nor widespread. It is difficult to decide whether it is the followers or the critics of progressivism who are the more riled by this finding. If the evil consequences of informal teaching are such-and-such, and then it is found that the causal factor was not activated, the blame rebounds on to the older methodology.

Two general observations are perhaps in order. In the first place, primary teachers have often mistaken content for method. There have been amazing changes in classroom technology, especially since the end of the Second World War, with much improved standards of design and presentation of materials and a veritable plethora of audio-visual aids in support. The 'interest' motif and a less formal regimentation have accompanied these changes so that many classrooms, superficially, look and sound quite different to those of pre-war days. What is less certain is whether the substantive knowledge about which the children are to be 'interested' or which they are to 'discover' or which they are to witness on the television screen is so different in character than in days of yore. Method is a second-order question: the first teaching question is why and what should the child be learning; the second question, that opening one resolved, is how best might the material be presented. It is likely that, to some extent, the colourful revolution in method has hidden the perpetuation of much of the content. To put it plainly, we may be in danger of teaching the same old rubbish more efficiently because of using improved techniques.

In the second place, what a more kindly and persuasive approach reflects is possibly more to do with a change in the social rather than the academic climate. Although there are, sadly, still some corporal punishment and other displeasing punitive features in primary schools today, what can be said with little fear of demur is that the primary classroom, for many children, is a pleasanter and cosier spot to be in than at any time in the history of schools. But this is a reflection of society itself, which is much more liberally inclined toward youngsters than at any other period in history. It is, of course, a circular effect. Since the turn of the century child and educational psychologists have gradually turned the adult mind away from an abrasive view of child-rearing, and the influence of such thought on teacher-training has been considerable. It is not a matter of arguing over who should take the credit for the improved atmosphere; it is a question of appraising teaching approaches in their social contexts. We should be no more surprised to find liberal, warm-hearted approaches in the twentieth-century classroom than to uncover paternalistic hectoring attitudes in its nineteenth-century pre-decessor. Nonetheless, it is pleasant to record that the major change in the elementary/primary pattern of education over the last 200 years has been social and relates to the quality of the relationship between teacher and pupil. Other changes may have been less dramatic, but that one is steadfast. It is probably true to say that an English primary school, operating on friendly but systematic lines, is one of the sanest institutions in English society today.

The array of fashions in child psychology, dating from the early years of the century, have been bewildering and volatile. *In toto*, they have contributed to this overall relaxation of the adult-child relationship; it is less sure that, as specific doctrines about the educational process, they have been deeply heeded. As one observes teachers of varying generation, it is difficult to differentiate in their practice under which dispensation they were trained. The Herbertian dogma of apperception and the five stages of learning; the American stimulus-response school of McDougall and Hall; Piaget with his concept of equilibration and the self-regulatory tendency of each organism—all have been expounded at inordinate length in the teachers' training cadres, but one can not often pick out the influence. Maybe it is cumulative, and educational psychology grows rather than oscillates. What is, however, much clearer is this more optimistic, happier view of the child.

To clarify the point by simple polarization, the 'little man' of James Mill, his mind a larder to be stocked, has been replaced by the child of Dewey and Piaget, his mind, like good wine, maturing slowly. One vital turning-point in that development was the publication of Lewis Carroll's *Alice in Wonderland* (1865) and *Alice through the Looking Glass* (1872). It is not without reason that the sagacious pundits of children's literature use *Alice* as the Christians use the birth of Christ or Moslems the Hegirah. Carroll's work separates dark from light. He promoted or, at least, epitomized the novel vision of the 'child-likeness' of children and the ideal of children being not only mini-adults but humans at a special and identifiable stage in their growth.

If one had to name a change as significant, vis-à-vis content and approach, as class-teaching has been for structure in the infant/junior years, it would be this one. What information and skills teachers are trying to impart in primary classrooms and the techniques they apply to this task have not changed much fundamentally. The changes have more often than not been in colour and style. The recognition of the child-as-child is the key feature, and it is fair to say that, even now, there are some teachers who find that recognition more difficult than others. A summary phrase to define what a hundred and more years of infant/junior teaching has produced by way of the typical primary teacher would be: Gradgrind tempered by the White Rabbit.

Essay subjects and seminar topics

1 Select a non-basic primary-school subject, such as art, physical education, geography. Trace its ancestry, attempting to note and comment upon its aims, materials, methods, and status on the timetable. Seek out points which have changed and points which have stayed the same.

2 Some years ago Princess Margaret opened a primary school in Barrow-in-Furness with an expensive and modern language laboratory for the teaching of French. According to *The Guardian*: 'the children spoke no word of English during the Princess' visit'. Discuss the implications of small children in Barrow not speaking English.

21 THE PRIMARY SCHOOL TODAY

Where disadvantage to the child appears there is always a case for displacement of the amateur by the professional. The dilemma runs deep in our society as between a commitment to the obvious advantages of upbringing in families and the different but no less real advantages offered by professional child care in all its forms. This dilemma expresses itself with particular poignancy in the case of children who grow up under the worst conditions of social disadvantage. The dilemma is, then, one between displacement of the amateur and support for him or her. On the whole, the traditions in professional education have been those of displacement, but the idea of the community school is one which embodies a movement towards support rather than displacement. It involves a more difficult and sophisticated professionalism than does the alternative principle.

Professor A. H. Halsey (1975)

Adequate school funding cannot, then, be justified on the grounds that it makes life better in the hereafter. But it can be justified on the grounds that it makes life better right now. This suggests that students' and teachers' claims on the public purse are no more legitimate than the claims of public highway users who want to get home a few minutes faster, manufacturers of supersonic aircraft who want to help their stockholders pay for Caribbean vacations, or medical researchers who hope to extend a man's expectancy by another year or two. But neither are the schools' claims any less legitimate than the claims of other groups.

Professor Christopher Jencks (1972)

A sketch of the primary school today emerges as an historical product from the preceding two chapters. It is, characterisically, a school arranged into classes, with the teachers pursuing a chiefly prescriptive approach, with considerably more social latitude than of old.

This is more than a personal observation. The portrait is largely borne out by Her Majesty's Inspectors' report, *Primary Education in England* (1978). This was undertaken among children of 7, 9 and 11 years of age in 1127 classes in 542 schools in England during the school years 1975/76 and 1976/77. It provides one of the most broad-ranging surveys of primary education since the Plowden Report of 10 years earlier.

On staff deployment, the report said, 'the predominant arrangement was for the class teacher to be responsible for nearly all the work of the class' — although the great majority of classes had at least one other teacher for music or sport or some other specialism. On approaches to teaching, the report concluded, 'of the teachers in the survey classes, 75% were found to use mainly didactic methods; 20% used a mixed approach; and 5% used a mainly exploratory approach. The report defined 'didactic' as 'inclined to direct the children's work in accordance with relatively specific and predetermined intentions, and explanations usually preceded action by the children'. 'Exploratory' was defined as putting children into 'the position of finding their own ways of solving the problems set', and 'explanations by the teacher usually accompanied or followed work by the children'. In a telling couple of sentences, the report recorded that 'in the great majority of classes, the content of work and use of resources was prescribed, sometimes to the extent that children had insufficient opportunity to incorporate information already known to them or make use of spontaneous incidents that arose. In only about one class in ten was there evidence of extended studies!'

As for the social climate, 'a quiet working atmosphere was established in the great majority of classes whenever this was needed' and 'consideration for other people and concern for the school environment were widely and effectively encouraged in almost all the classes inspected. In 90% of the classes teachers provided opportunities for children to take responsibility and to participate as members of a group. In about two thirds of the classes, situations were planned and used to encourage children to make informed choices, to use their initiative and to be responsible for their own work and behaviour.'

So much for the popular myth of the 'playway' do-it-yourself primary school of Fleet Street (and other) imagination. The Report also scotches the related fallacy that primary schools pay insufficient regard to the basic skills of the three 'R's and that standards are dropping in those aptitudes. 'Teachers give a high degree of priority to teaching basic reading skills', claimed the report. 'The use of graded reading schemes was universal in seven-year-old classes and nearly so in nine-year-old classes.' Indeed, HMI went on to criticize, not the basic mastery of the reading technique, but the 'tendency for children to receive insufficient encouragement to extend the range of their reading'. On reading tests, the average score of the 11-year-olds was 31.13 out of 60, consistent with a rise in standard since 1955 when the score was 28.71. The equivalent maths score was a satisfactory 27.97 out of 50, against a predicted mean of 25, although, once more, children 'would have obtained better scores if they had appreciated the general rules that underlie the large number of different mathematical examples they work in schools'. And, as a general comment, it was claimed that 'better than average scores in the reading and mathematics tests occurred in classes where the curriculum was broad'.

The inspectorate made several recommendations but spoke with 'optimism for the future', pointing to the fact that 'the personal relations are good and the children behave well'. Even allowing for that certain blandness which creeps into official surveys, it is a heartening picture, and yet a mysterious one. How has the belief developed and spread of easy-going primary schools, ignoring the basic skills, with a consequent dip in standards? How, conversely, has the belief developed and spread of exciting, open-ended, exploratory 'discovery' schools, extending the frontiers of children's experience in all directions?

The reasons are probably several in number, but they must begin with the change in social atmosphere already referred to, with which might be coupled the vivid technical additions to the teachers' weaponry. Moreover some of the few schools which, brightly and bravely, embraced the progressive cause attracted, fairly and rightly, plenty of publicity. The British progressive infant school became part of the itinerary of every visiting transatlantic or Australasian educator and each such school had a hallowed place in every college of education's hall of fame. It reached the point where headteachers of what they self-styled the old school could claim (I personally heard several) that they were the only head left using formal or didactic methods, and one was never sure whether they were misled or misleading. Assuredly the last of these particular Mohicans were as plentiful as the Sioux at Custer's last stand.

All this conspired to give a marked impression of progressivism run amok. In any event, the purported struggle between 'progressive' and 'traditional' or between 'informal' and 'formal' methods was ever a fallacious sidetrack. A truer test of teaching is whether it is 'systematic' or 'incidental', that is, whether (whatever the approach) it is pursued with rigour and consistency or not. There is, paradoxically, plenty of incidental formalism in schools. The 1978 report on primary schools, while noting that there were schemes of work in most schools for English, maths and religious education, reported that 'fewer than half the schools had schemes of work in any of the other subjects'. In many cases and in several subjects, children totter haphazardly from piece of work to piece of work, and from class to class, without any sense of development or increased grasp. The liberal approach of headteachers, leaving to individual members of staff the choice, outside of the basic subjects, of materials and work programmes, can end, for the children, in a kind of intellectual anarchy.

What appears to have occurred is a compromise between a regular approach to reading and maths and an irregular approach to practically everything else, and that has little or nothing to do with formal or informal methodology. If a child is studying, for instance, Richard Lionheart at the wrong time, at the wrong age, at the wrong level and in the wrong place, it matters not a jot whether he is copying down notes from the board, in serried ranks arrayed, as regimented as a Pomeranian Guardsman, or whether, swinging from the chandelier, he is 'discovering' about one of our four homosexual kings and producing a project.

But what is remarkable is the manner in which the public has accepted and fostered the myths about primary schools, and this raises the question of the public relations aspect of teaching. In a public opinion poll undertaken by the National Consumer Council at the time of the 'Great Education Debate' in 1977, while over eight out of ten parents were very or fairly satisfied with the performance of the schools their children attended, more than two out of five said they were not told enough about what methods were used and what subjects were taught in schools. The general good-will felt by parents towards schools, especially at the primary level, is very satisfying, but it ill-matches the particular complaint of parents about lack of information. A darkly comic instance of this happened in a survey of parents living in educational priority areas (1969) where equally high percentages (in the top 70s) were both highly pleased with the schools and utterly ignorant of what they actually did.

In 1977 the Department of Education and Science, urging 'that parents should have easy access to the sort of information which will enable them to understand their children's development. and help in their communication with the schools' published a circular containing 19 items 'which should be made available to parents'. The check list was as follows:

1 the name, address and telephone number of the school;

2 any special characteristic (e.g. single-sex, denominational);

3 names of the headteacher and senior staff;

4 how parents should arrange to visit the school and times at which the head, senior staff members, class teachers and year heads are normally available for consultation;

5 the number of pupils normally admitted each year;

6 the basis on which places are normally allocated;

7 special facilities offered in any particular subjects or activities;

8 arrangements for religious education;

9 (secondary and upper schools only) public examinations for which pupils are prepared, and the range of subjects and options available;

10 a brief indication of the normal teaching organization and of any special organization or methods used (including arrangements for teaching children of different abilities);

11 clubs, societies, extra curricular activities, including community service, normally available.

12 organization for pastoral care and discipline of pupils;

13 whether school uniform is required and if so the approximate cost;

14 whether any parents' or parent-teacher organization exists;

15 school journal, if any;

16 local school transport arrangements;

17 the lea's arrangements for the provision of free school meals;

18 the lea's arrangements for the provision of free PE kit and school clothing grants;

19 (secondary and upper schools) the lea's arrangements for the provision of Educational Maintenance allowances.

Secondary school items have been left in the list for general interest and to avoid confusion, and the 1980 Education Act promises substantive action in this important field, as part of its objective of improving parental rights and choice.

The transmission of information to the home, and the establishment of a two-way dialogue, is necessary and not only in the interests of improving public comprehension. There is the important professional point that, given the enormous bearing home background has on educational development, it is essential to form a sound working partnership with the home, so that parents might intelligently support what teachers are initiating in those few short hours the children are in school. There are now well-established modes for making contact with parents and keeping them fully informed about the progress of their children and the general organization of the school.

This overlaps with another issue regarding information. The last few years have witnessed some depth of public reaction to the practice of maintaining secret records. The United States, for instance, has taken considerable legislative steps to ensure that official information is much more readily available to the public, and compaigns have been mounted on this side of the Atlantic for similar objectives. In the education service, as in the health and social services, the meaningful point has been the maintenance of individual records. In a 1978 survey it was found that, despite the splendid lead of one or two authorities, hardly any lea allows parental access to all documents appertaining to their children. A quarter leave it to the discretion of the headteacher, usually a recipe for retaining confidentiality, while the overwhelming majority offer no rights of this kind to parents.

This is a very serious issue. First, it has a moral dimension. Such records or reports based upon them may be seen by other teachers, other schools, social workers, the police and potential employers. The ones who are categorically rejected are the ones they most concern — the parent and the child. Second, there is a real danger — as the research into record-keeping demonstrates — of gross inaccuracies being left unamended. Sometimes this is because family circumstances alter, and sometimes because highly-charged prejudices and opinions are included. Some authorities, in an attempt at objectivity, utilize complex forms, with teachers, for instance, having to produce profiles of children on, in one case, the basis of more than 130 questions. Teachers may have to mark pupils on obtuse scales for personality, more often than not without training or advice, so that giving a seven-year-old a quotient on the 'completely dishonest—absolutely trustworthy' spectrum begins to look quite hair-raising.

It is not so much the Orwellian fear of a conspiracy that is disturbing—it is the near-certainty that records are badly kept, and full of errors and oddball fancies. Records are an essential aspect of school teaching; it is their openness which is in question, and there are some teachers who would claim privacy of records is part of their professional remit, arguing that such reports are often too technical for the common herd. But it really is difficult to counter a compound of the moral view that secret records are odious and the pragmatic view that, without parental access, errors may be recorded and left unchecked for years.

All this does not detract from the judgement that English primary schools, while not so revolutionized as some have imagined, probably form that sector of the education system which most harmoniously combines personal contentment and personal development for the client. In many schools the mood has changed, so that the human relations between teachers and parents and children is possibly healthier than it has ever been. One does not suggest that, over the last 150 years, *all* state-subsidized teachers have been bereft of the milk of human kindness, but, on balance, the social climate of primary schools has improved. Teachers, now and in the future, should be seeking ways of building educational relationships on these pleasant social ones, inviting parents to participate more fruitfully, open up the dialogue, in terms of information and records, with much more generosity of spirit. Borrowing from the Hollywood of the 30s, the primary school's motto should not be Greta Garbo's 'I wanna be alone', but Mae West's 'come up and see me sometime'.

Essay subjects and seminar topics

1 How far do you agree with the general conclusion arrived at here that primary schools are rather more unchanging than not, save for their social atmosphere?

2 'Has little to say...home provides little stimulus for conversation.' (On a secondary school report, but filed when the child was six.)

'Child slightly epileptic, possibly very backward.'
(The non-medical *opinion* of a teacher on a ten-year-old.)

'She is growing tomboyish, and is getting interested in motorbikes.'
(On the *medical* notes of a 13-year-old child.)

'Help'
'Manacles!'
(Each of these single-word statements was the sole comment in the concluding section of the separate record-cards of two young secondary pupils.

Discuss — then plan a Primary School record-card which would be valuable for teachers and parents.

SECONDARY SCHOOLS

22 SECONDARY SCHOOLS AND THEIR STRUCTURE

Alexis Still I have made some converts to the principle that men and women should be coupled in matrimony without distinction of rank. I have lectured on the subject at Mechanics' Institutes, and the Mechanics were unanimous in favour of my views. I have preached in workhouses, beershops and lunatic asylums, and I have been received with enthusiasm. I have addressed navvies on the advantages that would accrue to them if they married wealthy ladies of rank, and not a navvy dissented!

Aline Noble fellows! And yet there are those who hold that the uneducated classes are not open to argument! And what do the countesses say?

Alexis Why, at present, it can't be denied, the aristocracy hold aloof.

Aline Ah, the working man is the true intelligence after all.

W. S. Gilbert *The Sorcerer* (1877)

The grammar school must be a starting-point of any description of the separate education of secondary as opposed to primary schools. The grammar school was an admirable, and a peculiarly English, contribution to the northern renaissance, meeting as it did the urgent Tudor call for architects, navigators, agricultural surveyors, accountants, merchants, clerks, legal and administrative officials and those other occupations which suddenly became important in the sixteenth century. It is claimed that, at peak, there was a grammar school for every 6,000 of the population: at the time of its brief renaissance in the first half of the twentieth century, the ratio rarely bettered one to 50,000. This secular device to man the maritime, trading and managerial ranks of the Tudor State was aptly summarized in Thomas Elyot's *The Governor*, most noted of Tudor educational treatises. Latin was the staple, but this was not as antiquated as it sounds, not in a nation where that language was still widely used in legal and other circles.

Eventually a few of these grammar schools became patronized by the rich and ennobled, adopted a boarding dimension, and later accepted the label of public schools ('public' meaning 'endowed' as opposed to 'private' schools). Wryly, these—Charterhouse, Christs Hospital—had often been intended for those of lowlier origin, or—Harrow, Rugby—for local boys. By the end of the eighteenth century, Eton had earned itself the reputation of England's most eminent school, and these 'great schools' thereafter pursued a course which only occasionally crossed with that of a developing maintained system. Many boys attended such schools after private tuition locally, usually at home, and there were many who enjoyed their entire, often broader schooling at home. Despite the import of private tuition and the general decay of education in the eighteenth century, the public school emerged into the nineteenth century to luxuriate in the rigid class consciousness of that age, and with the *nouveaux riches* and aristocracy vying for places. With headmasters like Arnold of Rugby and Thring of Uppingham, these schools built up solid reputations, some of which still remain intact.

The grammar schools had either less luck or worse management. They became impoverished in resources and style, and found themselves outmoded by urban and industrial conditions. The once powerful Leicester Grammar School, over 300 strong, degenerated until, in 1818, it had one boarder and three day boys. Their formalism and restrictiveness was suffocating—Lily's Latin primer, published in 1515, was widely used. By the 1830s there were little more than 100 grammar schools left with less than 3,000 pupils. They were challenged by the private academies (Warrington is regarded as the most notable) where the sons—and later the daughers, albeit in separate schools—of tradesmen and others were catered for with an increasingly non-classics syllabus, one more in keeping with the realities of Victorian middle-class and business life.

However, for the majority of children, secondary education was non-existent and so it remained throughout most of the nineteenth century. The School Boards attempted to fill the vacuum, partly by offering extra-elementary subjects of a technical and scientific nature, and partly by offering instruction to older pupils. By 1897 'payment by results' had been modified, with a block grant, based on average attendances, replacing the individual subsidy for each 'passed' scholar, and this allowed some indulgence in manual and technical subjects. A standard VII, one over the normal six, was introduced, and, with Birmingham in the van, Higher Grade and Higher Elementary Schools were opened. In 1892 the school leaving age rose to 12. The Department of Science and Art encouraged these moves with grants, and the demand for subjects like cookery, botany, chemistry, shorthand, engineering and book-keeping grew and was largely met. To take one instance, the Salford School Board ran classes, often self-supporting, in subjects like animal physiology and applied mechanics. In 1890, the Union of Lancashire and Cheshire Institutes examined in 20,000 art, commercial and science subjects. In 1900 there were nearly 200 Schools of Science in the country.

Unluckily, this impetus for commercial and technical education was halted by the 1902 Act which obliterated the Boards. Apart from the political and religious controversy involved (see chapter 13) there was another kind of vocational pull—for solicitor's clerks, pupil teachers, local government officers and the like. Nor was the work of the School Boards unvaryingly attractive; it was as often tedious and narrow, and there were many humanists who rightly recalled Matthew Arnold's dictum that a technological without a liberal education was mere 'fizz, fizz, bang, bang'.

Robert Morant and his supporters were bitterly, if sincerely, opposed to the School Boards' 'excessive emphasis' on technical education. A staff inspector and colleague of Morant's, J. W. Headlam, prepared a biting indictment of the School Boards' endeavours in the post-elementary field, and Morant used this as a platform for pressing for his 1904 Regulations for Secondary Schools. A timetable was prescribed of not less than 4½ hours each for English, geography and history; 3½ hours to one or two languages, with Latin obligatory if there were two; and 7½ hours science and maths, including at least 3 of science, but with the accent on the theory. Thus the traditional 'literary' curriculum won the day, as the county councils took up the cudgels of secondary education for the first time.

Although the School Boards made only feeble and sometimes illegal efforts, there were still, in 1895, 250,000 children over 13 in some sort of schooling, at a time when there was no properly organized secondary education and only four out of 1000 children had a chance of a grammar school place. Then there was a resuscitation of the grammar schools. In 1904 there were 491 grammar schools with 85,000 pupils; and in 1925 there were 1,616 with 334,000 pupils.

At this stage 'elementary' was not the same as 'primary'. It was a type of education, which ran concurrently with the revamped grammar schools. With the Part III authorities able to supervize elementary education until and beyond the school leaving age, a number of neo-secondary schools appeared. There were the all-age schools, where children stayed in one school throughout their careers; and then there were the higher elementary schools, the central schools and the junior technical schools. By these means a kind of para-selective secondary education evolved, with clever children, both fee-paying and non-fee-paying going to grammar school, and the rest gradually finding, usually to the age of 14, some other form of instruction. Just before the First World War 4% of youngsters were in grammar schools; just before the Second World War, it had risen to 11%.

It was the 1944 Act which rationalized the administrative aspects by erecting a unitary system. The 'elementary' category was banished and all fees likewise were abolished. The primary (up to 11) secondary and further education stages were introduced, and the local authorites were left to organize their own secondary schools, with official advice in numerous reports, like the 1938 Spens Report, the 1943 Norwood Report and the 1943 White Paper on Educational Reconstruction, to help them. What emerged, although it was never legislated for as such, was the famous tripartite secondary system of grammar, technical and modern schools with 11-plus selection the modern label for the older 'scholarship' examination. These were supposed to equate with the Norwood Report's hypothesis of three differing 'aptitudes'—the scholarly, the technical and the 'essentially practical'—by which children might be grouped.

In many ways, this was a retrospective analysis, based on the kinds of schools in which youngsters found themselves, to wit, the grammar schools, the junior technical schools and the higher elementary or senior schools, respectively. The educational advice surrounding the implementation of the 1944 Act was, therefore, founded in practice rather than theory. It beatified what existed. In reality, in was a bipartite system. The grammar schools continued to be important, although they did not grow in numbers. There were 1,300 (700,000 pupils) 20 years after the Act was passed. There were barely 200 technical schools at that juncture, and they soon began to dwindle, but there were 4,000 secondary modern schools (1,500,000 pupils). In summary, the secondary system of grammar schools for about one in three pupils, with the rest elsewhere, was developed in the inter-war period, and merely revitalized and co-ordinated in the post-war phase. Both kinds of schools could, of course, trace their ancestry beyond 1902, but the post-1902 era was the critical one for the structural character of secondary education.

Although the notice-boards and titles might have changed after 1944, it was obvious enough that the buildings, teachers and curriculum usually remained steadfast and unchanging.

By this time the ideal of the comprehensive school was fast becoming prominent. It was, of course, to become a party political issue, with the Labour Party as pro-comprehensive, as, 100 years earlier, the Liberal Party had been pro-School Board, and, once more, the Conservative Party espousing the traditional grammar school. There were so-called bilateral and multilateral schools to begin with, and then the belief in a common or non-selective school grew. Initially, it was experimental or in areas—Anglesey, for instance—where it was convenient so to proceed. By the 60s many Labour-controlled authorities were, in spite of aggressive protestations, producing comprehensive schemes. In the famous Circular 10/65, issued when Anthony Crosland was Secretary of State, the Labour Government elected in 1964 requested leas which had not done so to draw up such schemes, 'to end selection at 11-plus and to eliminate separatism in secondary education'. It became a political hot potato, with the Conservatives withdrawing the circular in 1970, the Labour Party passing the 1976 Education Act to bring recalcitrant authorities into line, and the Conservatives, in turn, repealing that legislation in 1979. By the end of the 70s, however, 'reorganization' had taken place almost everywhere, with just a few backsliding authorities, of which Tameside became most notorious, hanging back. In 1979 2,900,000 pupils (83.4%) were in comprehensive schools.

The impetus behind reorganization came from two sources, social and educational. The social factor was the growing awareness that the grammar school was predominantly *bourgeois* in character and clientele (School Certificate and then GCE might be defined as awards for clerkly diligence) and that its divisiveness was cultural as well as intellectual. The much vaunted 'parity of esteem' was never affirmed in terms of resources or prestige. The secondary moderns, perhaps missing a chance of developing an exciting new form of education, limped painfully in the wake of the grammar schools. Educationally, the chief assault on differential secondary schooling was aimed at the unfairness and inefficiency of selection at 11. A 10% error either way (which each year, must have meant many thousands of mistakes) was thought to be the nearest possible approach to the ideal, while, in 1959, a test of recruits for national service, when still compulsory for all 18-year-olds, revealed that nearly one in four had been misplaced or mis-streamed on selection at 11. It is probably fair to say that, in the late 60s, the mood of public opinion was anti-11-plus, but uncertain about comprehensive schools.

Two points further need to be considered. The comprehensive

school, of itself, cannot and does not remedy gross social inequalities, and these continue to dictate much of how children perform in school. Either externally, with areas of a particular social cast determining the character of the local school, or internally, with some schools streaming intensively, that problem remains. The 'open access' sixth form has had some success; in the mid-70s a survey by Guy Neave suggested that one in eight of the comprehensive school pupils studied who went to university would not have passed their 11-plus. But, in general, the school remained a weak rather than a strong factor in socio-economic selection.

The trend towards comprehension follows, as we have seen, an historical route. Gradually, the 'commonalty' of schooling has risen through the age-ranges, as first one and then another type of selection has been abandoned. There was, initially, secondary education for only a few, and then, as more children were thus indulged, there was selectivity. As the school-leaving age has risen to 16 and as increased numbers have remained in school at 18, a division at 11 has become more and more irrelevant. Some authorities have attempted to meet this by forming middle schools, up to 12 or 13, or junior high schools from 11 to 15 or 16. It is a truism to state that all primary schools are comprehensive, but, ultimately, therein lies the justification of the common school; that, socially and academically, distinction between categories of individuals is misleading and unproductive.

Essay titles and seminar topics

1 Comprehensive schools, with their underlying egalitarian impulses, are sometimes accused of 'social engineering'. Why is this so, and is it true? Is any form of secondary school organization, such as the separation of academic wheat and chaff 11, open to the same accusation?

2 Trace the lineage of one or more secondary schools within your experience, commenting on the social or political factors which led to shifts in its (their) fortunes.

23 SECONDARY SCHOOLS: CONTENT

The tide which begins to rise in the veins of youth at the age of 11 or 12. It is called adolescence.

The Hadow Report (1926)

Policeman (discovering boy and girl locked in passionate embrace down back-entry)

'What game d'you call this then?'
Boy (obviously satisfied by his activity)
'I dunno, but football and cricket's had it'.

Anon.

In historical terms the secondary school, apropos its internal dealings, faces one crucial problem, that of adolescence. Although many, since the time of the Hadow Report, have drawn attention to that rising tide, much of the consideration has been given to its symptoms or consequences and, curiously, not to its fundamental character. Over the last 90 years the school leaving age has risen from, for many, 11 to 16 or 18. During that time the adolescent tide sweeps in, and, however defined, it seems that it is arriving earlier. Biologically, the onset of puberty appears to be retracting. Whether this is due to healthier environs and nutrition or to some mysterious swing in the genetic pendulum seems uncertain, but, for instance, the sanitary towel is no stranger now to the primary school. Socially, a less restrictive and more pluralistic society, with television and other media in constant action, means that children come to an earlier and more enlivened awareness of life's riches. Conversely, one's initiation into adult life is postponed. A longer education, is followed, for increasing numbers, by several years of post-schooling or, indeed, unemployment, and by, for many, a later start in parenthood— many people are well into their 20s before assuming what are regarded as the normal responsibilities of the adult.

It is well-known that, in many societies, initiation into the world of work and marriage is much more abrupt, with special ceremonies to monitor the occasion. In our possibly more complex civilization there is now an extremely wide gap between the first sensations of adolescence and the final commitment to career and family. It is a veritable no-man's land, with its denizens seeking, often vainly, for emotional, psychological and sociological identity.

Several years at least of this phase are spent in school, and it is important to note that the school, historically, was created for pre-adolescents. The school leaving age has been raised over and again over the years, and, basically, we have casually by-passed that vastly significant watershed, the onset of adolescence. One enters school at five and stays in a similar institution until at least 16. Although there are differences of approach and style in the secondary school, it remains structurally an institution established for children, with the entire regimen devised to that end and supervised by those in authority on these terms. The critical difficulty for the secondary school, therefore, is the fact that many, possibly the majority, of its customers are not children but young adults, and that, trapped by the accidents of educational history, it is deemed necessary to treat them as children.

The incidence and traits of this problem vary immensely. In some schools in some districts it breaks forth as indiscipline, to the point of violence and excessive truancy. Elsewhere it may emerge as boredom and frustration, with schools unable to retain the interest and confidence of the pupils. In other schools one has the impression that pupils are using the school, eager to pick up its examination and other rewards, but resentful and scornful at the same time. The tedium and disruption is by no means total. Many schools and many students are successful in all senses. But one's overall impression is that compared with the primary school, the secondary school is neither so happy nor industrious.

At the time of the ROSLA pilot projects in the early 70s, several headteachers and others claimed to be planning a fifth and final year which would be 'real, exciting and relevant'. There were sceptics ready to observe that, had the first four years been such, there would have been less to worry about in an additional fifth. Radical curriculum developers were disappointed to hear from secondary school-children that, despite the new found colour of their wares, colleges of further education, perhaps with traditional and narrow courses, were frequently more attractive. Their ambience was more adult. The basic question to be considered is whether the 'school' as originally envisaged and presently organized, is the proper place for young adults, beyond the age of 13 or so, to be. The alternative would appear to be some kind of 'community college' for those over 13 or 14, and catering for all those currently in further and adult education. It is a difficult problem because many teachers would point to the lack of intellectual and emotional maturity in these young adults, whatever their physical and social ripeness. Nonetheless, the whole question of how secondary schools should be organized and how related to the rest of the education system has been insufficiently debated.

There have, however, been ceaseless discussions on almost every other aspect of secondary schooling, and it is proposed to comment briefly on some of these arguments.

First, as to buildings, the later development of secondary schools has led to their decided advantage in terms of age over primary schools: Only 600 of England and Wales' 5000 secondary schools open in 1975 had pre-1903 accommodation: 90% had some building dating from 1946 or later, with the rest mainly having been built between 1903 and the start of the Second World War. Reorganization has resulted, however, in the administrative disadvantage of the split-site phenomenon, with 20% (36% in Greater London) of the schools on two or more locations, with over 300 suffering sites with half-a-mile or more between them. 650 schools have no playing field within a quarter-of-a-mile. Occasionally, school building projects have been launched to meet the needs of secondary reorganization. In 1978/79, for example, £20,000,000 was set aside for 130 such projects, although it is worth noting that this formed part of a general programme of works to relieve unemployment in the construction industry. In 1978 the government admitted that it would cost the prohibitive sum of £1,500,000,000 to correct all the deficiencies and meet all the requirements of comprehensive reorganization, and the lack of such resources remains a chief grouse of those unwilling to accept the notion of comprehensivization.

Second, as to size, there has been criticism of the gigantic and thus, in the view of many, impersonal nature of many secondary schools, one in five of which have over 1200 students. In the November of 1978, the then Secretary of State, Shirley Williams announced a virtual ban on schools of more than 2000, of which there were but 15, the last of them being approved in 1973. There are about 250 with 500 to 2000 on the roll. Her suggestion was that the ideal is six, seven or eight forms, fewer than that endangering the range of sixth-form options.

This concern with the viable sixth form has long been at the hub of the 'size' debate, a debate recently revitalized by the effects of a lowered birth-rate on secondary school rolls (see chapter 9 for other details). Early in 1979, the Chief Education Officer for Manchester, Dudley Fiske, pointed to the 33% fall in the secondary school registers from 4,000,000 to under 3,000,000. This suggested that the average comprehensive school, with about 1000, could shrink to 600 and even to 450, with deleterious consequences for choice of subjects. Given that there is and, increasingly, would be emphatic opposition to closures and amalgamations, he advocated using curriculum as the key, so that by loosening the rigidity of pupil-teacher ratios, a broad range of subjects might be maintained. Other proposals include the use of sixth-form colleges or schemes which sixth formers might attend in different schools for different subjects, to ensure that specialisms might be economically taught.

There are hopes that the sheer increase of space in secondary schools will help with the problem of discipline, for which some blame, in part, overcrowding. Bullying, vandalism and hooliganism are troubling certain secondary schools, and special behavioural units have mushroomed. There were 300 of these in 1977, catering for some 4000 pupils, most of them over the age of 14. These units soon earned the colloquial title of 'sin-bins' and many of them were quite detached from the school they were intended to serve. As always, questions as to whether these are reformative or punitive, or whether just plain dumping grounds, have been raised, but they are certainly a far cry from the hour's detention of the traditional school.

Third, as to performance, the secondary schools, like the primary schools, have been attacked in the *Black Papers* and elsewhere for lax standards. It was part of the Conservative defence of the grammar school and the direct grant list to mourn their passing in terms of their high academic levels. (The direct schools were those 170 odd quasi-independent schools which, in return for a direct grant from the government, and considerable outlay by local authorities, offered a goodly proportion of free places to the bright: the system was abolished during the 1974-79 Labour government, but the Conservatives are introducing individual grants—the assisted places scheme—for clever children of poorer means to attend independent schools, as several Conservative councils already do).

The purportedly liberal mode of mixed ability teaching has come under fierce attack, and an inspectors' report of 1976 did seem to imply that this was not unwarranted. As with so called 'progressive' primary methods, the chief criticism was that it was often inefficiently done or was something else done under the mixed-ability flag. In any event (as with primary progressivism) six out of ten schools used no mixed ability classes at all, and only two out of 100 used it until 'O' levels—it is a device utilized by not too many schools and then just for the first year or two. What has happened is that the old 11-plus argument has been reintroduced as a streaming-versus-mixed ability squabble. The pragmatist tends to opt for 'setting', with children moving from group to group according to their aptitude in different subjects, or 'banding', in which children are placed in broad, sizeable and none-too-rigid ability groupings.

Examinations remain the critical test of the secondary school, despite the complaints of several commentators that they are unreal and unfair, and should be replaced by continuous assessment and pupil profiles. Examinations remain a symbol of the influence of Victorianism on our educational institutions and, although the tune changes (from Matriculation to School Certificate, then, in 1950, to General Certificate of Education, with later the Certificate of Secondary Education, and now with other changes in the air) the melody lingers on.

In the event, examination results do stand up to scrutiny, unless one accepts the next step in the traditionalists' argument that exam standards themselves are dropping. In 1977 80% of school-leavers, compared with 50% in 1966, gained some form of educational qualification, and, over the same period, 50%, rather than 33%, obtained one or more 'O' level passes. Over 1,000,000 candidates took 'O' level in the summer of 1977. Candidates taking CSE and

GCE examinations in 1977 showed an increase in 90% on the 1967 figures. With over 250,000 each taking CSE exams and 'A' levels, the total number of candidates in 1977 was well over 1,500,000. A comparison of 'A' level results as between 1977 and 1962, when there was only a handful of comprehensive schools makes interesting reading:

1962: 59,400 pupils (9% of age range) passed one or more 'A' levels and
47,700 pupils (7% of age range) passed two or more 'A' levels.

1977: 117,000 pupils (15.5% of age range) passed one or more 'A' levels and
93,000 pupils (12.5% of age range) passed two or more 'A' levels.

Approaching twice as many school-leavers therefore obtained 'A' levels at the later date, something of a tribute to the comprehensive system, but, inevitably, one must sound the warning bell about the vast difference in performance according to social background.

More children, obviously, are remaining at school to take such examinations, and that, too, is partly to the credit of the comprehensive school and its nursing of the late developer. It also reflects the anxieties of the labour market, and that most pressing of problems, youth unemployment. There have been various projects aimed at improving the secondary curriculum, notably the Social Education Project sponsored in Nottingham by the Schools Council in the late 60s. As in primary education, the intention of curriculum developers has been to produce a more relevant and less alien syllabus, but, should, as some prophesy, youth unemployment remain a constant, another critical issue presents itself—it brings us full circle to the central problem of the adolescent. The general thrust of the secondary school is to prepare for a life centred on the work-place, and the Protestant work-ethic is frequently invoked. In future, much more attention may need to be paid to preparation for unemployment or, to put it more positively, leisure. Whatever else, the education of the adolescent always seems to be in some state of crisis and the HMI Report of December 1979 *National Secondary Survey: Some Aspects of Secondary Education in England* is a useful and encouraging starting-point for any current study of the problem.

Essay subjects and seminar topics

1 The use of 11 years of age as an educational dividing line is largely accidental. Discuss its drawbacks and advantages and offer

alternative structures to cater for the education of the adolescent.

2 Buildings—size of school—performance, particularly in exams— these are three issues with which secondary schools are concerned. From your experience of a given secondary school, comment on how these issues contribute to the ethos or otherwise determine the character of the school.

24 SECONDARY SCHOOLS TODAY

Schools serve primarily as selection and certification agencies, whose job it is to measure and label people ... this implies that schools serve primarily to legitimize inequality, not to create it

Christopher Jencks *Inequality* (1972)

Educationalists are realizing more and more that children leave school essentially with what they brought into it; the influence of school in promoting 'equality' is so limited as to be almost non-existent

Hans Eysenck *Black Papers* (1975)

The effects of school process and balance of intake on examination successes are much greater than the effects of parental occupation and about half as powerful as the child's own ability level

Michael Rutter *Fifteen Thousand Hours* (1979)

There are, today, about 4,000,000 secondary pupils, approaching 80% of them in comprehensive or non-selective middle schools. The grammar school population is down below the 250,000 mark and selection at 11 obtains now in only a handful of authorities, despite some occasional signs of reneging in staunch Tory authorities. As chapter 22 demonstrated, the twentieth-century reincarnation of the grammar school has been in historical terms dramatic and short-lived, although the adjective 'traditional' is often used to describe it. Now for the vast majority of children, a common end-on system of primary and secondary schooling is available. Some 30% of these children stay on, beyond the statutory school leaving age, although it must quickly be added that the number of 18-year-olds is very much less. Predictably, 75% of these children aged 16 to 19 are from professional families but only 15% of children of similar age from unskilled workers' families are in full-time education. Of the 750,000 1977 school-leavers, 83% had (as the previous chapter noted) at least one graded examination success, about 10% had five or more higher grade 'O' levels or CSE equivalents, and about 8%

succeeded in three or more 'A' levels. As for destination, 550,000 went directly into employment, and 155,000 transferred to a variety of further and higher education agencies, a ratio of nearly four to one. So much for a static snapshot of the recent situation in secondary schools. Those bare statistics, however, tell nothing of the fiery emotions engendered when secondary schools are argued about. Most of the *causes célébres* of modern education (the William Tyndale tempest excepted) concern secondary schools. A firm suspicion abounds in some sections of the media and of the populace that the comprehensive school breeds violence, subversion, indolence, indiscipline and low standards of scholarship. The supporters pooh-pooh this as wild and overgeneralized, pointing up the view that, where schools have these unpleasant traits, it is the reflection of a flawed society.

We are immediately flung into the swirling maelstrom of the 'nature-nurture' argument. It is probably true that, in the past, schools and teachers have made extravagant claims about their capacity to effect change in their clientele, so that it is scarcely surprising that, when delinquency, vandalism, apathy and unrest are discerned, detractors are only too ready to lay the blame for that on schools. A minor illustration of this occurred in 1978 in a well-publicized row over the publication or not of examination results, with some pressing for the case for on the grounds of necessary public information, and others the case against on the grounds that social factors made a nonsense of any interpretation of the raw scores. My own modest contribution (*Guardian*, 3 October 1978) to the discussion was a proposal to publish the results along with some commentary or monitor of the social factors. This seemed to me a proper recognition of the cyclic nature of the school-society bonding, each in turn influencing the other (see also chapters 4 and 8), and it appears that some such compromise might emerge from the 1980 Education Act which specifically calls on schools and leas to yield up information to parents. The school does not create society in the school's image; but the reverse is not entirely true either, for school is a part of, and not apart from, that society. The relationship is circular, not see-saw, in shape.

Strangely, the extreme wings of the environmental and hereditarian schools of thoughts have both dwelt on the importance of the school. For Jencks and James Coleman and their ilk, background, especially home, is the key, while for Eysenck, Arthur Jensen and Cyril Burt (whose work has recently fallen under the gravest suspicion of not being genuine) genes are the Open Sesame. For Illich, and other de-schoolers, the school is thus no more than the puppet tool of an oppressive society, and, for the *Black Paper* tribe, a highly elitist, selective and part-independent system is the rational and self-justifying structure conferring proper reward upon superior genetic combinations.

An important third school of thought, represented by Professor A. H. Halsey, has always urged that opposition to either of these stances does not and must not automatically imply espousal of the other. Especially during the late 60s and early 70s, many critics of the schools agreed that the social background of the pupil was paramount, but maintained that the schools were at fault in misusing the marginal influence they retained. By and large, they affirmed rather than combatted the dictate of the outside world. The famous Wiseman research prepared for the Plowden Report suggested that home and neighbourhood factors outmatch school factors in the ratio of 82 to 18 on a 100-point scale. That is almost a ratio of four to one; but it is not five-none! The school has 20% of the influence available on that reckoning, and this should be meaningful and have more effect than it does.

The publication in 1979 of *Fifteen Thousand Hours* by Professor Rutter and his associates very rightly made a forceful impact, and, as a survey of current secondary schooling, it quickly won a richly deserved prominence. Based on a most thorough investigation of 12 South London Comprehensive Schools, it has re-presented, in telling fashion, the case for the school being alive, well and influential. Its results have been broad ranging enough for their utilization as the proof for differing theses, according to, as Harry Judge amusingly wrote, whether your newspaper was likely to be read in Bournemouth and Solihull or Hampstead and Cambridge. There was, it was claimed, solace for the proponents of both a disciplined and a liberal approach.

What the report did not claim nor its authors suggest, despite some reviews to the contrary, was that schools could equalize the educational disadvantage consequent upon social disparities. What, in a distinguished and forthright manner, it did propound was that a 'good' school will improve the behaviour and attainments of *all* pupils in similar degree, and a 'bad' school, vice versa. In short, how a school operates in what might be called the Wiseman margin may make or mar a pupil's education and thus life-chances.

Given the starting-point of pupils' ability at entry, occupation of the family breadwinner and a behavioural profile, the secondary school careers of the 3,500 students surveyed varied enormously. Academically, the average exam performance (except for the least able children) in the most successful school was as good as that for the most able children in the least successful school. Indeed, the best school was shown to be about four times as successful, in examination performance, as the worst. In terms of behaviour, attendance varied from about 12 to 17 out of a possible 20, after adjustment for social features; the schools with discipline problems were not necessarily those importing the largest groups of 'difficult' children from primary schools, and the best school was five times better than the worst school.

After 'controlling for intake', the probabilities of 'official delinquency' (that is, children cautioned or found guilty, in a juvenile court) were three times greater at the worst than at the best school. What is more, the patterns of success and failure were similar: for instance, a well-attended school is likely to have well-behaved pupils doing well at exams.

Where Michael Rutter then went further was in examining what made for these truly startling differences and his cannonade left several brave and popular figures dead or mortally wounded on the educational battlefield. For it appeared that many of the administrative tales beloved of both teachers and parents, were superficial and irrelevant. Several matters which have generated much heat in educational circles have apparently shed but little light. The casualty list included: whether the school was single-sex or co-educational; whether it was a mammoth 2,000 strong or a frail 400 on roll; whether it was voluntary-aided or state-controlled; whether it was spacious or cramped; whether it was on one site or many; whether it had a year or house system for pastoral care; whether it was an ancient or a modern building: even pupil-teacher ratios and resources seemed to have little effect, although, in truth, these were fairly generous in all schools. As an added bonus, the split-site schools did as well academically as the one-site establishments, and their pupils were better behaved. Nor did some schools just have more efficient teachers than others, while another old favourite, continuity of teachers, came unstuck, having no effect on attendance or results and, oddly, finding itself linked with worse behaviour.

Having disposed of the myths and part-myths, the Rutter team identified two major elements in the making of the successful secondary school, although, given the small number of schools researched and their close geographical incidence, it has not been possible to allocate precise proportions of credit to each of the dynamic duo. The first relates to the ethos of the school, and the degree to which it is well-organized, encouraging and caring. It was not so much traditional methods which paid off, but traditional values of teacher dedication, commitment and preparation. As was argued in the primary school section (chapter 20) it is not so much whether a school uses formal or informal, but whether it uses systematic rather than incidental methods. Frequent praise, much more than frequent punishment, was another aspect of this, with schools using corporal punishment, officially or unofficially, seeming to *produce* bad behaviour. Schools which, in the liberal mould, heaped responsibilities and opportunities for participation upon their students, showed improved behaviour, attendance and examination results.

The second, and the nearest to a political element, was the discovery that a balanced intake was a prerequisite of the successful school. Other considerations having been taken into account, it was demonstrated that a fairer proportion of high ability children raises the performance and behaviour of all children at all levels of ability. Sweet music to the ears of comprehensive propagandists—it would seem that this very positive influence operates by means of the relationships between the pupils themselves.

This finding could and probably will affect the debate about secondary organization two ways. In the first place, it implies that the co-existence of grammar schools with comprehensive schools—or policies to syphon off bright 'state' children into independent schools—would be damaging, so real is the need for a balanced intake. In the second place, if such a balanced intake is a principal means of raising secondary school standards, then its promotion might have the consequence of limiting that other political runner, parental choice. As a matter of fact, Professor Rutter examined the relation between parental choice and school behaviour and performance, and found no links at all. This suggests that schools do not do better when parents dearly want to send their children there, and that parents are not much good at choosing the right schools for their children. Although several commentators on *Fifteen Thousand Hours* made play with the fact that the man-in-the-street commonsensical view about schools being different was confirmed, they omitted to mention that the man-in-the-street was distinctly unskilled at spotting exactly what the differences were!

Now, of course, there may be other reasons, moral and social, for calling for co-educational or smaller or voluntary or one-site schools. There seem, too, to be powerful reasons for educating and informing parents more profoundly so that their choices can be shrewder and more perceptive. Nonetheless, and at a time of much rhetoric and insufficient reason in the continuous row over secondary school organization, the work of Professor Rutter and his colleagues offers a salutary and substantive credo for secondary school management in the last 20 years of this century.

Politicians, parents and administrators are called to task by an analysis such as this, but it is teachers, above all, who should take careful and practical note. Sadly, within weeks of the report's publication, there were teachers' leaders ready to begin contrary announcements, with sentences starting 'whatever academic researchers might think...' or some similar phrase. In the past, there has been a tacit and understandable agreement among teachers that their endeavours and the organization of their schools are more or less on a par. In the theatre, actors take the praise for a triumphant play and the author or producer takes the blame for a miserable flop. In schools, teachers enjoy the credit when things are successful, but tend to find the children and their families culpable when they go wrong. At best, they have insisted that their professional judgement must be honoured, but there are various ways of skinning the cat, and headteachers and staffs must seek their own road to salvation. But if class size and additional resources are not, possibly, of consequence, if a systematic approach is preferable to a more spasmodic one, and if a tolerant, openhearted mode is more beneficial than an abrasive, critical one—then teachers must somehow come to terms with these factors. They must begin to accept that professional decisions of these kinds cannot be left to individual whim and prejudice, but must be assessed according to the latest state of our knowledge of these matters.

Essay subjects and seminar topics

1 At a conference in Glasgow, a Scottish head said 'over many years I have been successful at producing honest and trustworthy and hardworking young people—but I would never let the school become involved with the community, where the values are dishonesty and laziness'. Comment on the implicit paradox in this statement, and suggest how school and society might become better reconciled one with the other.

2 Drawing on your experience of one or more secondary schools, attempt to measure its (their) strengths and weaknesses, using Michael Rutter's findings as criteria.

POST-SCHOOL EDUCATION

25 THE POST-SCHOOL YEARS

I perceive now that the real charm of the intellectual life—the life devoted to erudition, to scientific research, to philosophy, to aesthetics, to criticism—is its easiness...it's incomparably easier to know a lot, say, about the history of art and to have profound ideas about metaphysics and sociology, than to know personally and intuitively a lot about one's fellows and to have satisfactory relations with one's friends and lovers, one's wife and children. Living's much

more difficult than Sanskrit or chemistry or economics. The
intellectual life is child's play; which is why intellectuals tend to
become children—and then imbeciles...it's much easier to be an
intellectual child or lunatic or beast than a harmonious adult man.
That's why (among other reasons) there's such a demand for higher
education. The rush to books and universities is like the rush to the
public-house. People want to drown their realization of the
difficulties of living properly in this grotesque contemporary world,
they want to forget their own deplorable inefficiency as artists in life.

Aldous Huxley *Point Counter Point* (1928)

Beyond the school-leaving age the provision of education grows
somewhat confusing, although, truth to tell, it concerns a minority
of the age-range. To begin with there is what Shirley Williams once
called 'the broken bridge', those years between 16 and 19 when the
passage from youth to the adult world must be negotiated. An
increasing number do, of course, stay on at school beyond the
statutory leaving point. By the mid-70s, 25% of the age range (about
278,000) were sixth-formers, and it is expected that this will rise to
33% in the coming years, peaking at 335,000 in 1984, and settling
around 325,000 in the 1990s. Actual sixth forms have remained
much the same size—70 or 80 in strength because it is the number of
schools with such luxuries which has grown. The sixth form is now
less élitist than it was, with rather more students topping up their 'O'
level qualifications than was the rule, and this adds to the constant
problem of sixth forms—viability. Many argue that a sixth form
needs to be 100-strong to enable a reasonable range of options to be
maintained, with a dozen or so available for each 'A' level group. The
point made in chapter 20 about flexibility (for example, joint classes
made up from different schools) must be heeded if provision is to
remain efficient.

Some 10% of the same 16 to 19 age-range—approaching
200,000—pursue what is now rather awkwardly called non-
advanced further education. Of these 33% follow GCE courses, 25%
do City and Guilds courses, another 25% are on technical, commercial and similar courses (for ONC/OND or TEC/BEC exams, etc)
and the remaining 17% take internal college courses. This type of
provision does not figure high in the status stakes, with local
authority grants on a discretionary as opposed to an obligatory base,
as in higher education. They tend to fall into the long but rather
sombre tradition of the Mechanics Institutes of the Victorian era,
offering earnest and worthy instruction to the working class. The
assault on technical education (see chapter 22) in the early years of
the century left it with few resources and little kudos, despite the
efforts of the Junior Technical Schools and other agencies. Between

the wars and in the immediate post-war years it was night school which soberly provided technical and commercial qualifications.

For those who missed out on the grammar school and for those who did not excel themselves there, the night school was the straw at which sociology's equivalent of the drowning man—the frustrated, aspiring parent—clutched. Re-titled 'evening classes' and increasingly concerned with adult education proper, they still offer this sort of facility. In my own memory of family members dancing attendance thereon, it was an invitation accepted but grudgingly. It seems that, now as then, a contradiction exists between employers complaining of poorly-motivated young people and employees, free from the shackles of schooling, unwilling to undergo further formal instruction. Some of this same difficulty exists in terms of day release. Only 20% of 16 to 19-years olds going straight from school to work obtain or desire release for additional education, and not all of this is popular with either employers or employees.

Something between 300,000 and 400,000 young people take up employment each year, and the great majority do so without an opportunity for further training either at work or on release to further education colleges. However, these are probably better off than the several thousand currently unemployed. Because of education's accent on the work-ethic and because of its peculiarly daunting effect on morale at the onset of adult life, youth unemployment is critical in psychological as well as in socio-economic terms. Through the welter of schemes sponsored by the Manpower Services Commission, from April 1978 onwards, huge funds have been expended on giving some form of work experience or training to all school leavers. By the Easter of 1979 this had just about been realized, although the stop-gap artificiality of such endeavours needs to be borne in mind, and such schemes were increasingly to come under attack from the newly-elected Conservative Government of 1979.

Beyond the immediate school-leaver group, the adult education banner waves bravely. Unfurled in the Victorian era, when useful knowledge was required by many, it has survived all manner of shot and shell, and, while bedraggled at times, remains valiantly flying. Adult education embraces a number of elements, such as the Worker's Educational Association, founded in 1903 and nowadays subsidized by public funds, or the extra-mural departments of the universities. Increasingly the Adult Education Institutes of the local education authorities have made the running, and the scope of adult education has widened considerably. It comprises education in prisons, the adult literacy scheme, work with immigrant populations, liaison with community development groups, and so forth. The lines between further and adult education are of course blurred, but overall, it is safe to estimate that about 3,500,000, which amounts to approximately 10% of the adult population, attend some such class annually. Aims vary—some adult education is trenchantly punchy in its political character, its objective the increased awareness and capability of the working class. Much of it is more benign, its aim no more exciting than to initiate suburban housewives into the urbane mysteries of flower-arrangement or continental cookery. It is likely, nonetheless, that adult education will be the chief growth-point for education in the future (see final chapter).

It is interesting to compare the age groups in the broad pattern of further education in England and Wales, including the now declining teacher-training section and also youth clubs.

	under 21	over 21	total
Full-time and sandwich courses	329,000	167,000	496,000
Part-time day release and other part-time day	409,000	297,000	706,000
Evening only	170,000	517,000	687,000
	908,000	981,000	1,889,000

The figures are for 1977 and are taken from major establishments only. They indicate that almost 50% of such education is concentrated into the immediate post-school phase, with only evening classes showing a higher proportion. This is predictable enough, but it demonstrates how little adult, as against youth, provision exists. Less than 500,000 over 21s are enjoying any form of daytime education. The breakdown in general shows that 500,000 are on full-time or sandwich courses, nearly 1,500,000 are on part-time courses, and 1,750,000 are enrolled at adult education and youth centres. Interestingly, 2,000,000 of this 3,500,000 are women, chiefly because of the two-to-one ratio of females in adult education.

Such an analysis clears the ground ready for a commentary on the Afrika Korps of post-school education, namely higher education. Higher education is, in a sense, the most ancient form of institutionalized schooling extant. The foundation of Oxford and then Cambridge as the English prototypes of that eminently medieval agency, the university, the community of scholars, is well-known. Alone they reigned supreme for centuries. Their clerical origins—a Cambridge newspaper headline during the university's rowing competition once read, 'Jesus Bumps Lady Margaret',—are obvious enough, and have proved very influential. The ideals of the cloistered pursuit of truth and of classical scholarship, rarely distracted by the real world, were preserved, but there was also the elitist notion of Oxbridge providing a finishing-school for the rich and powerful. Despite many changes in recruitment and grant-awarding, half the Oxbridge entry is still from the public schools, which cater for but a handful of the population.

It was not until the nineteenth century that, with an enlarged population crammed into large cities and successful industrialists and merchants ready to finance local enterprises, a succession of universities was formed. In 1828 the beginnings of London University were established and Durham and Manchester soon followed.

By the First World War there were a dozen or so new universities, but, typically, there was little advance on this between the wars. It was after 1945 that the major expansion began, so that nowadays scarcely any region or major conurbation lacks its university. They are as symbolic as the old style cathedral. There are now 44 universities, including the Open University, and 30 polytechnics.

Using the term 'higher education' to cover full or part-time courses in advance of 'A' level or its equivalent, there were in 1978 500,000 full-time or sandwich and 250,000 part-time students. This total of 746,000 students is overseen by 64,000 staff, half of them in the universities, where over half the full-time students are enrolled. Expenditure in 1976/77 was £1,300,000,000, about 20% of the country's educational budget.

What the experts call the 'age participation rate' has naturally risen rapidly with the extension of provision. Around the end of the 50s a little less than 7% of 18-year-olds moved on to higher education, but during the 60s it practically doubled, levelling off around 13%, with about 100,000 18-year-olds annually starting higher education courses. Two subsidiary points should be considered. First, although the numbers have dramatically risen, the social class fractions have scarcely altered. The proportion of working class children going to university is much the same as it was in the 1920s, so that higher education remains mainly a middle-class preserve. Second, the decline in numbers which, in turn, is affecting primary and secondary education will, by the 1990s, cause problems in the highest echelons. The maximum number of 18-year-olds— almost 1,000,000—will occur in 1982, but there will be a fairly savage drop to 650,000 by the mid-90s, and this will lead the universities and polytechnic authorities to think furiously.

One special factor will presumably figure in that thought process. The clerical inheritance of 'withdrawal' for study and contemplation has had two far-reaching consequences. Not without some justification, this has often meant a refusal to come to terms with the vocational needs of modern life; indeed 20% of Oxbridge graduates pursue advanced courses, many of them hopeful of an academic post. This scholastic purity has led to a situation where, it would seem, graduates, particularly the more talented ones, have been reluctant to take jobs in industry or otherwise disport themselves productively. This is not intended as a slight on the hundreds who enter the professions or administration, but, in 1979, less than 200 went into industry.

The other aspect concerns residence. The monastic basis for Oxbridge, the withdrawal into a communal life for a lengthy period, had its practical side. Commuting from, say, Carlisle and Plymouth in the fourteenth century was not a workable proposition. The notion of the residential university has, however, persisted, in the face of motorways, highspeed trains, a prolific incidence of institutions and amazing advances in audio-visual techniques. 'Leaving home' is used constantly, especially by students, as having some form of educational benefit, but, while this may be true, there seems no reason why a small segment of the age-group should be feather-bedded to do so. Other 18-year-olds 'leaving home' have to make shift for themselves.

There is little doubt that the enormous cost of higher education, a goodly part of it devoted to expensive, static equipment in non-vocational subjects and to halls of residence, refectories and so on, will be looked at askance if numbers and demand drop. Some polytechnics have tried to become more oriented to the twentieth century, and the Open University has given a fruitful lead in the development of correspondence and audio-visual media. The universities have tremendous status and respect and, of course, their protégés become the leaders of opinion and of government. Nevertheless, there may be pressure to moderate the historical position of higher education in favour of a more directly vocational provision and a less residentially-founded ethos.

Essay subjects and seminar topics

1 Is it, as Aldous Huxley says, easier to be an intellectual child than a harmonious adult man? Is further and higher education a means of postponing decisions about real life?

2 First primary schools and, more recently, secondary schools have become 'comprehensive', at least in the sense of a common structure. Post-schooling preserves a dualism, with further education playing secondary modern to the university/polytechnic grammar school. Should there, could there, be a tertiary common or comprehensive structure?

26 THE EXTRA-SCHOOL DIMENSION

R. H. Tawney's Equality *contains a lampoon of what he calls 'the Tadpole Philosophy'. In it he attacks the suggestion that 'the presence of opportunities by which individuals can ascend and get on, relieves economic contrasts of their social poison and their personal sting', drily commenting, 'as though the noblest use of exceptional powers were to scramble ashore, undeterred by the thoughts of drowning companions'.*

The struggle of many tadpoles to become a few frogs, one of nature's multifarious cases of many being called and few chosen, does appear to illustrate our education system only too aptly. It has been called an education for frustration, as, at various levels on the uphill grind, groups of the climbers from among the huge party who started the travail are sloughed off, and only a tiny number emerge at the summit, replete with their university degrees. A university degree does not confer happiness automatically, but an extended education does offer a wider choice of careers, life-styles and the like. On balance, more rather than less education is a 'private good'. Whether or not it is also a 'public good', in the sense of the better educated making larger contributions to the commonwealth, is less certain; but adhering to the private stance, it is difficult not to conclude that the competition for education is real and earnest.

What seems to have emerged in modern times is an uneasy counterpoise of liberty and equality. There is the wish to give everyone, regardless of class or creed, an equal opportunity to benefit from educational facilities, along with a desire to offer individuals freedom to soar as high as they will. This is set alongside the view that such liberty allows for that individual self-fulfillment and such equality provides for that general communal good which together form the basis of a social democracy. The humble talents of the miner's son are not wasted; there is equality of opportunity; he becomes an accountant or surgeon; he thereby realizes his personal ambitions and gives generously to the common good at one and the same time.

Professor A. H. Halsey has often pointed out, notably in the Reith Lectures of 1978, that the triple concepts upon which modern western democracy was formed include fraternity as well as liberty and equality. No one doubts that this grand visionary trio is full of contradictions. Each must vie with the other two for supremacy and, presumably, the ideal social democracy might see the threesome pulling with equal strengths and providing an equitable tension. It is probably fair to state that, thus far, liberty has been in the ascendant, with equality battling hard but well-behind in second place, with fraternity bringing up the rear, a poor third.

Translating this into educational terms, one might surmise that equality of opportunity, in the technical sense of resources made available to all children has been approximately attained. The actual distribution of these resources is, however, subject to fierce competitiveness with, by and large, accessibility ruled by success and not failure; in other words, distribution is unequal, with the gains going to the victor. This is a predominantly libertarian device, for, if equality reigned, all children would be treated in similar degrees as, arguably, more time and money would be expended on the less clever in the belief that their needs seem to be the more urgent. Add to this the effects of home and environmental background on a child's capacity, and freedom to use the education system (as against equality within it) appears to be paramount. What of fraternity?

Fraternity involves mutual affection and a self-effacing regard for one's fellow-men. Its postulate is that no man is an island, and that we are or should be an interdependent people. Its caring ethos is a psychological and moral grade above the collective self-interest of, say, paying rates for the fire brigade lest our own house catch fire. That brand of negative contractual insurance is important and respectable and has due ethical standing, but it somehow lacks the personal commitment of the truly fraternal society, where, in togetherness, each is eager to raise the general heights of fulfillment and endeavour. Transferred to education, and reduced to its simplest terms, the primary-school class, combined together in a joint project, is acting fraternally, while the secondary-school form, each pupil attempting to better the marks of his confrères, is not.

Liberty and equality in education have a fuller significance when observed in their community setting, with the school seen as an agency for both. It offers freedom of choice and access to children that in conjunction with their parents, they might disport themselves more convincingly in the community. It provides some uniformity of service that each pupil might have some education to assist him in coming to terms with his community. In these ways the school serves its community, defined both locally and nationally. A 'fraternal' service would consist of activities which underpinned the collective social consciousness, again of either the immediate host environs or society at large. Many schools, albeit often indirectly, do just this. In many districts the school is the social hub, a centre which coordinates local action and clarifies local opinion. The village school is the most romantic illustration of this, but there are many other schools in a variety of areas which do likewise.

Unluckily, the tradition of the English school does not easily lend itself to the pursuit of brotherhood. The 'factory formula', in its architecture and imagery as well as its objectives and methods, saw to that. The school was developed, as was described in chapter 19, more as a treatment centre for its individual clients than as a focus for social coherence and action. This might also be regarded as a corruption of the ancient clerical heritage (illustrated in the preceding chapter by the Oxbridge and boarding school convention) of withdrawal. This rough-hewn mix of the clerical, the industrial and also the military led to a policy of incarceration, with the pupils herded fairly unceremoniously into the closed environment of the school. The intense professionalization of the teaching force added the last barrier in the encirclement, ensuring that the professional-lay dialogue of teacher and child normally occurred in seclusion from the home and the rest of the community.

A salutary irony is that the Victorians, masters of the 'closed' institution like the factory, the school and the workhouse, were also champions of the 'open' agency. The music hall, the department store, the seaside resort, the spectator-oriented sports arena for football or cricket—these are but a few instances of Victorian inventiveness. The distinction, of course, is that the one category was for social delinquents or casualties or for the harsh realities of brutalizing labour, while the other category, colourful and breezy, was about profit and pleasure. Much as schools may try to be outgoing and in touch with their locale, it will require a gigantic *volte-face* in the thinking and planning of schools to procure a fundamental open-ness in their processes.

Would such a radical lurch toward fraternity be warranted? When the idea of the open school as a social entity or focus is pressed, it is often argued that this would incommode the more straightforwardly individualistic efforts of the school, the liberty-equality quotient, so to speak, with its emphasis on the pupil's personal attainment. Two 'fraternal' features might compensate for any such deprivations. The idea of a 'relevant' curriculum gells with a communal approach. Child development, in the minds of several commentators, is best nurtured by reference to the concrete experience which the pupil finds in everyday life, while the skills and knowledge he requires are frequently concerned with a similar cast of day by day reality. Then there is the growing belief that, because the home is also an influential educational determinant, the teacher should be intimately concerned with parental involvement, and, in turn, parents would often feel most confident in coping with a community-oriented curriculum.

Those two features, both with liberalizing and equalizing

qualities, have already begun to affect the evolution of the community school.

Ideally, the community school is a fraternal school. It operates for and on behalf of its host community who should, preferably, accept a marked responsibility for its well-being. It should provide an education service, in the widest possible sense, to all members of the community; it should encourage their involvement, and especially that of parents, in the academic and social life of the school; and through such devices as the governing body or the parents' association, it should oblige the community to participate in the school's management. The Conservative Education Act of 1980, with its clauses on parental choice, information for parents and statutory parent governors, should be of considerable value in this regard.

The classic precedent for this newer tradition of 'inclusion' as opposed to seclusion was Henry Morris' seminal efforts to develop the village colleges in Cambridgeshire in the 1930s. Since the Second World War two frequently separate strands have evolved. The 'use of plant' argument with its authentically economic ring, has been influential in some areas, notably where there have been redevelopment schemes or new towns. Shared amenities, like the refectory, the sportsdrome, the library and the drama workshop, have made good commercial sense where large secondary complexes have needed to be built, and they provide a solid core for community development. The 'community colleges' of Leicestershire or Coventry and other authorities sometimes offer a freewheeling service by day and in the evenings, and for much of the year round. Some of these have gone further by evolving a more socially conscious curriculum or by proffering joint classes to children and adults. Particularly in the post-Plowden era, it is the primary schools which have chiefly pursued the second thread, that of home-school relations. Obviously, the import of parental participation is more essential at the infant and junior stages, and there have been many bright and enterprising ventures by schools to reach out and embrace the home more effectively. Much of this is of a social kind, which is not unimportant, but it lacks the bite of those pioneer attempts which have invoked the aid of parents in the direct teaching process.

Notable examples of community schooling are, in effect, to be found in the pre-school world. Home-visiting schemes and mothers' cooperatives, along the lines of Home link in Liverpool or the Scope groups in the Southampton area, are robust illustrations, while the entire playgroup movement, at least where mothers join together in the general management and daily supervision of the group, is a splendid example of the genre. These often come full circle, with the parental activities within the pre-school frame adopting the character of adult education. In its turn, adult education has loosened its shackles a little, and has begun to see itself more as the lubricant of the internally combustible action of local communities; hence, for instance, the 'outreach workers' of authorities such as ILEA.

As is often the case with the history of English education, the movement toward a more extrovert form of schooling is sporadic. One authority will have developed a beneficial scheme of parent governors; another a worthwhile approach to home-school relations, and so on. With Coventry and one or two others as honourable exceptions, no local education authority, let alone the nation at large, has developed a grand strategy for all levels and interpretations of education vis-à-vis the community. It is by no means certain that the change to the open or community school will be completed, despite the strong advances made. It should be stressed that this credo of the school as the catalyst for social coherence and brotherliness is a revolutionary one. The vested interests of the present, fortified by the entrenched interests of the past, will make its realization difficult.

Judged by the long record of educational history a likelier scenario will be that teachers and others in authority will select pragmatically from the 'community school' articles of faith, and impart into their practice those items which might be seen, in the short-term, to be of value. It is in this fashion that shared usage of plant, on economic grounds, and home-school relations, for sound professional reasons, have both made some headway. It is not yet possible to assess whether, in the next 20 or 30 years, such spasmodic inroads might extend sufficiently to the point where, in time, they could amount to an overall change in the character of the English school.

Essay subjects and seminar topics

1 Choosing a school of your acquaintance, try and assess how far it has journeyed, if at all, in the transition from the conventional 'secluding' to the community 'including' school.

2 If liberty, equality and fraternity are indeed the watchwords of a social democracy, how far is the efficient running of a school, in terms of its pupils' academic aspirations, compatible with them?

27 THE FUTURE

When the Royal Navy, many years ago, threatened mutiny the First Lord of the Admiralty, Sir Thomas Trowbridge, offered a solution to the Cabinet. They should, he proposed, hang a hundred or so lawyers. The Cabinet were astonished and—their number including the Lord Chancellor and other legal dignitaries—dismayed by this tangential approach, and asked for an explanation. 'Fellows on the lower deck who can read' was the First Lord's definition.

The struggle to stop what is loosely called the establishment seeing education in the same light continues. It could be argued that only as much education is 'released' to the people as is compatible with the stability and sustenance of society. Governments seem to be both attracted and horrified by education, regarding it as necessary for vocational and civic purposes but as alarming if it appears to liberate any over-excitable impulses in the people. At best, it has been viewed (and in this it is similar in almost all other civilizations) as the preparation of the young for the norms and rigours of adult life. It is the induction process by which junior members of society are transformed into law-abiding, God-fearing senior ones. Let us be optimistic in these final pages, presuming that education might come to have a total dimension, serving all persons at all times that they might have constant self-realization.

We have long been obsessed with the 'apprentice-bound' concept of education, identifying it strongly, for all but a small minority, with what happens to children in schools. The analogy of the car petrol tank has occasionally been used to illustrate this, with each pupil's tank filled once at the onset to a level and of a grade over which he has little control; and then he travels along the motorway of life with varying degrees of sluggishness over a varying range of distance, with only a few allowed access to the occasional service station. The alternative concept of 'recurrent education' has excited some attention over recent years. This visualizes education as a life-long process, recognizing that 'because experience is life-long, access to educational knowledge must be also' *Recurrent Education* (1974). To sustain the analogy, it proposes that the access to and availability of a wide variety of filling-stations should be everyone's right. This 'new kind of citizenship right' was succinctly defined by the Canadian Worth Reports of 1972 as follows: 'it grants a claim on schooling to each individual according to his own lifestyle and his preferences for patterns of work and leisure. It is intended to provide each person with a means to participate in the shaping and continuous re-shaping of his environment and his society'.

The possible application of such a concept to our society is apparent enough. Given the rapidly changing nature of economic technology and the social dislocation wrought by structural unemployment, the need to provide a much greater *variety* of vocational and leisure education is becoming all the time more necessary. This goes beyond the 'second chance' provision for adults which is often remedial and inevitably suffers in comparison with the splendid delights of higher education per se, but it has been foreshadowed by the efforts of some secondary schools to make their classes available to adults and by some of the recommendations of the Russell Report—for example, the creation of Local Development Councils for Adult Education 'widely representative of those who have an interest in adult education as providers or users'.

In the splendid phrase of Professor Tom Stonier of Bradford University 'the dole must become a sabbatical': put another way, this envisages a 'National Education Service' which, at all times and for all ages, offers a creative and open-ended opportunity for citizens to improve both their contribution to society (for instance, as work people) and the quality of their own lives (for instance, through extended *leisure* pursuits). This would help us realize that twin hope of *equality* of educational opportunity for an amalgam of individual well-being and communal betterment.

If one word had to be earmarked to summarize what is required it would be 'flexibility'. If we are to consider a major reform in the education system along the lines of increased choice then we must, at the very least, correct the perspective. Unless there is a much greater elasticity of types of provision and availability, it would probably be unwise to contemplate a mechanistic change purely in the character and control of schools. We might end with a dynamically changing society served by a static, cemented schools system.

What steps, then, might be taken toward constructing an education service that would, as well as being responsible to consumer need and protective of basic social rights, look forward to the twenty-first century?

If it is agreed that education should be a lifelong process, one might, in practice, begin with the time-factor, one curiously omitted from much of the educational debate since 1944. Equality of opportunity, to confer real meaning, should embrace equality of time, otherwise the requirements of access and availability fall at the first hurdle. Equal opportunity then masquerades as a uniform and obligatory schooling for 11 years, with a brief preface of nursery education for some and a lengthier postscript of up to nine years for others. The maximum time-opportunity available to students now in the United Kingdom is about 20 grant-aided and heavily subsidized years. Its recipients are, by this token, well-placed to choose advantageously among the widest range of career and leisure proposals in the land. It is well-known that the higher the education the higher the cost. The average expenditure on a university student is eight times that on a primary school pupil (see chapter 11). It is not denied that many of these beneficiaries make worthy contributions to society at large, although it is salutary to recall that over half of those who have enjoyed higher education remain in the education industry. But what is urged is that, unless everyone has similarity of access, the dictates of social justice and social productivity alike remain unserved.

Could one consider a model based on the principle that what society currently agrees is practical for some might be attainable by all? Let us suppose that, as a birthright, each infant be credited with a minimum of, say, 22 years educational provision: 11 years to be expended, as normally, up to 16, and 11 years, minimally, to help one negotiate one's route to that final educational experience, the grave, presaging, as it well may, some form of eternal 11-plus selection.

To borrow, one hopes not too aptly, from the old penal code, this would mean 11 years without the option, and 11 years with the option. And the second post-school category would carry automatic eligibility for tuition fees and an 'educational salary' based on the average earnings for the particular age-group, current income, family needs, or some similar set of criteria.

At the heart of this proposal is a desire to de-institutionalize education, to turn aside from the preoccupation with massive capital outlay, to concentrate on people and free ranging equipment and materials, and to encourage the dispersal of a network of educational facilities throughout the fabric of every community. The student would be able not only to select where and how to utilize his optional years merely in terms of their educational function, but also to remain engaged in the decision-making methods relating to that function.

In effect, each link in this learning web could become some form of student-tutor co-operative. These would vary enormously in size and style, but they would have in common that degree of user-sensitivity. Some, for instance, might be less 'participatory' than others: a group of students might elect to abdicate their decision-making rights, in part or whole, to a professional, but that would be their privilege so to grant or rescind. Similarly, a student might opt to split his time between two or even more agencies, according to his perception of his need. Others might determine to educate themselves or perhaps their children, at home, again in whole or in part, and should then be able to cash in their credit, with suitable safeguards, for educational materials. Some parents might choose to combine the roles: giving up work to self-educate and child-educate simultaneously, and claiming tuition fees and an 'educational salary' accordingly. That might be particularly attractive to the mothers of small children, for it should be borne in mind that this civic right should not apply only to those in paid employment. For some parents of young children a scheme whereby they could combine to form mother-child educational cooperatives would meet both the economic and social motivations which urge young mothers to seek often uncongenial employment.

It might be helpful to outline a possible lifetime's educational profile. Young Tommy Atkins might stay on at school for two extra years, receiving, it should be noted, an educational salary thereby. He then expends one year's credit over two years part-time, doing independent study and some light work or community service the rest of the time. Then he goes into full-time employment, still with eight years provision at his disposal. At 23 he feels a two-year course in his chosen career might be beneficial, so he is able thus to improve himself vocationally. At 42 he discovers that the opportunities in his profession are diminishing and that, in any event, he is rather jaded with it. He chooses to do two things end-on. An enthusiastic amateur ornithologist, he decides to indulge himself in a year's cultural pursuit of that admirable recreation, and, afterwards, to attend a year's re-cycling course for a trade for which fresh opportunities are appearing. At 51, with his daughter aged 16 keenly interested in archaeology, he decides to spend a year, alongside her, on an archaeological project. Before his retirement, he tops this up with a year's medieval history course and a year's house maintenance course, and, well into his 70s, the ageing Thomas Atkins feels that it would not be inappropriate to expend his last piece of free education on a year's study in comparative religion and ethics specially programmed for the senior citizen.

To risk no offence on sexist grounds, the parallel profile of Mrs Atkins is recorded. She takes a normal two-year sixth-form course and then a three-year degree-course, followed by the external part-time higher degree which, over four years, involves an expenditure of the equivalent of one credit. Five years remain to her. In the interests of family equity she spends a year studying civil engineering with her sixteen-year-old son when in her late 40s, and, in the interests of family harmony, she unselfishly joins her husband on his house maintenance pre-retirement course, but, baulking at the medieval history, she enjoys a drama activity and appreciation workshop for a year. Aged 70, and rather less gloomily contemplative than her spouse, Mrs Atkins uses her last two years studying for a degree in sociology.

Now there are those among you who may regard this as a fanciful caricature. There may even be those among you who echo the sentiments of a member of a Select Committee of the House of Commons to whom I gave evidence about the merits of recurrent education, and who would refer me to Tennyson's *The Lotos Eaters*. I was called upon to contemplate the divisiveness of a society in which some strap-hang grimly to their tedious labours whereas others bask in an Arcadian pasture of origami and flower arrangement. That politician had to be reminded that the precedent has been created. Roughly one in ten of the immediate post-school cohort fall into the following category: this group is unemployed and they live on means-tested benefits; incidentally, of the 40 odd means-tested benefits available this one has by far the largest take-up; some 100% compared with 62% for rate rebates. But no disgrace hounds them. They enjoy, by and large, high status and material comforts. They are called university students—and they are characterized thus not to be carping, for one would not wish to change their lot unduly, but to recall that there are already those few who enjoy cultural and leisure opportunities, alongside scholastic opportunities, and perhaps the gates of this educative heaven should be either wider or left unlocked longer.

However, it is always irritating when Tennyson is deployed to call one back to the line of dutiful realism, and there might be little political mileage in preaching the dignity and grace of an open access system of education. It is hard to think of an occasion in the chequered narrative of the history of education where the beauty of Academe outwitted or outflanked the beast of necessity. One must, then, point the gun of socio-economic expediency rather than wave the banner of educational parity.

Since 1945 we have been told that automation would bring leisure, and now (as we saw in chapter 5) in 1979, we have over a million at leisure, but, because of a dislocation in our forward planning, it doesn't seem to be the right million. When one is told that it would be costly to provide a positive programme of lifelong education, one should retaliate with the fact that unemployment, social security payments, government expenditure on training, and losses in taxation, are costing the country something approaching a colossal £10,000,000,000. Now, with the micro chip, so to speak, on everyone's lip, one hears sombre prognostications of 4,000,000, and 5,000,000 unemployed in the mid-1980s.

To this must be added another and more startling phenomenon. For the first time in the history of Western Society, a larger number of retired people are surviving. As chapter 7 outlined, they now compose 20%—some 10,000,000—of the population, and there are firm reasons of a social, let alone a moral kind, for responding positively in adult education terms to this feature. There is no need to melodramatize: one does not foresee gangs of old-age-pensioners roaming the streets mugging defenceless teenagers, but it does seem that an educative vacuum needs to be filled.

All of this may be set against the present decline in school-goers, granted the falling birth-rates of the late 60s and early 70s which are currently causing havoc in many schools. Let us examine a projected portrait of an age, circa 1990. It is possible that the schools population could have dived from its 9,000,000 peak of the mid-70s to as few as 6,500,000, and, allowing for the most generous estimates of the country's virility and fertility, should no radical alterations have occurred, about a million in some form of post-school education. There are likely to be 9,000,000 non-working women, to be collated with at the very least the 10,000,000 retired, and, on some analyses, 4,000,000 to 5,000,000 registered unemployed. That would leave about 15,000,000 still at work, doubtless wondering whether to regard their position as favourable or otherwise.

These are macro-figures, bristling with 'ifs' and 'buts', but the major point is to try and emphasize that less than 50%, and possibly as few as 40% of the population will be working in 1990. Incredibly, retired people already outnumber school children. The social strain of this transformation will assuredly make itself forcefully felt, and sooner or later, some form of custodial structure may well be developed, as in the past, to meet it. .

Now, and in the mid-term future, the emphasis will be more on the adult and less on the child than has been the case over the last 120 years. It will be the task of the Open University and of other like-minded education agencies deliberately to seize the opportunity to ensure that (as has not always been the case in the past) the education offered those adults in educational 'custody' is of superior quality.

The intention in proposing the 22-year blueprint for educational credit was not to offer a finished, polished schedule, but to remind that, as the history of our education service shows, although its broad frame may be determined by social and economic dictates, the significant character of its substance, which is so important to its individual students, is frequently at the behest of those who spot and take the initiative. The battle will go, as the American General said of his nation's Civil War, to those who get there 'fastest with the mostest'.

Essay subjects and seminar topics

1 The chasm between the Trowbridge thinking (that readers make troublesome 'sea lawyers') and the vision of constant educational refurbishment for all is a wide one. Is it possible to bridge the gap and how best might this be accomplished?

2 The motif of these commentaries has been that the education system is largely determined by socio-economic factors, with considerable internal detail dependent on individual initiative, accident, chance and Acts of God. Is this a fair balance? Can, for instance, individual teachers make much of a dent on the system and change it in any way?

179

Further Reading

In an overall survey such as this the objective is to stimulate thought and discussion on a wide range of items. One hopes this will lead readers and students to look more closely at some of the topics under review, and, as an aid to this, a bibliographical summary is herewith included. Other books have, of course, been mentioned in passing which should be of value. It is by no means exhaustive, but it does offer some suggestions for further study in most of the areas considered. First of all, a general suggestion. J. Lawson and H. Silver, *A Social History of Education in England* (1973) is very well worth referring to for most topics raised here—it is an admirable and complete social history of the country's educational system—and S. Maclure *Educational Documents 1816-1963* (1965) is an excellent compendium for continual reference.

EDUCATION AND SOCIETY

In terms of the general perspective of the growth of education, R. H. Beck, *A Social History of Education* (1965); T. L. Jarman, *Landmarks in the History of Education* and E. D. Myers, *Education in the Perspective of History*, (1960) might be recommended. Those wishing to place English education in its own political and socio-economic setting might consult E. J. Hobsbawn, *Industry and Empire*, vol. III of the Pelican Economic History of Britain, 1750 to the present day (1968); A. J. P. Taylor, *English History 1914-1945 (1965)*; E. P. Thompson, *The Making of the English Working Class* (1968) and S. Barraclough *An Introduction to Contemporary History* (1964).

Turning more especially to the history and development of English education proper, there are several splendid volumes. Among these are A. D. C. Petersen, *A Hundred Years of Education* (1952); J. W. Adamson, *English Education 1789-1902* (1930 reprinted 1964); T. Morrish, *Education since 1800* (1970); B. Simon, *Studies in The History of Education 1780-1870* (1960); H. C. Barnard, *A Short History of English Education* (1947); and for a briefer account, the author's *Nineteenth Century Education* (1970). Lastly, in this little section, a particular mention of W. H. G. Armytage *Four Hundred*

Years of English Education (1964): a most valuable work.

From the more purely social angle, and including the important issue of population, the following could prove useful: (ed) E. Butterworth and D. Weir, *The Sociology of Modern Britain* (1970); G. A. L. Lowndes, *The Silent Social Revolution* (1937); M. Young and P. Willmott, *The Symmetrical Family* (1973) HMSO, *Population and the Social Services*, Central Policy Review Staff (1977) and *Social Trends*, Government Statistical Service (1979).

Then there is the whole philosophic question of education's role in society. P. Freire, *Pedagogy of the Oppressed* (1970); I. Illich, *Deschooling Society* (1971); (ed) R. and B. Gross, *Radical School Reform* (1969); A. S. Neill, *Neill, Neill Orange Peel* (1972); C. B. Cox, R. Boyson *et al. The Black Papers* (1-5) (1969-77); A. Hopkins, *The School Debate* (1978); Schools Council, *Enquiry I: Young School Leavers* (1968) and E. G. West, *Education and the State* (1965)—these put the various viewpoints trenchantly.

The subject of the social composition of the school population is throughout a critical one. Few books could provide a balance of factual detail and lucid commentary: A. H. Halsey, *Educational Priority* vol. i *Problems and Policies* (1972); C. Jencks *et al. Inequality; a Reassessment of the Effect of Family and Schooling in America* (1973); I. Reid, *Social Class Differences in Britain* (1977) and G. Taylor and N. Ayres, *Born and Bred Unequal* (1969); for the most up-to-date and compelling analysis, A. H. Halsey, A. F. Heath and J. M. Ridge *Origins and Destinations* (1979) is now available.

For a follow-up to the social topics raised in chapter 9 there is (ed) F. Field, *Education and the Urban Crisis* (1977); (ed) J. Raynor and J. Harden, *Cities, Communities and the Young* and *Equality and City Schools*, Open University Readers (1973); A. N. Little, *Educational Policies for Multi-racial Areas* (1978) and R. Rogers *Schools under Threat: A Handbook on Closures* (1979).

EDUCATION AND THE STATE

Of course many books from the first section would be of value for further reading in this and indeed the third section. The same applies, in natural converse, to the books about to be mentioned.

Two or three books are particularly helpful on the growth and current structure of the English education system. These are R. Armfelt, *The Structure of English Education* (1961); P. H. J. H. Gosden, *The Development of Educational Administration in England and Wales* (1966); Ministry of Education, *Education 1900-1950* (1951) and M. Smith, *Church and State in English Education, 1870 to the Present Day* (1964). Such studies might be assisted by the political and social slant provided by R. C. Birch, *The Shaping of the Welfare State* (1974); H. Finer, *The Theory and Practice of Modern Government* (1950); K. Polyani, *Origins of our Time: The Great Transformation* (1945) and P. Gregg, *The Welfare State* (1967).

Finance is of vital import. R. Bacon and W. Eltis, *Britain's Economic Problem: Too Few Producers* (1976); D. Byrne, B. Williamson and B. Fletcher, *The Poverty of Education* (1975) and Chartered Institute of Public Finance and Accountancy, *Educational Statistics: Actuals* (annual) provide, from their respective corners, the further succour needed. Elliott Jacques, *A General Theory of Bureaucracy* (1967) and M. Weber, *The Theory of Social and Economic Organisation* (English translation 1947) are valuable interpretations of the managerial patterns one finds in educational administration.

On the local government side, readers might wish to try E. Eaglesham, *From School Board to Local Authority* (1956); J. Mann *Education* (1979); Association of Metropolitan Authorities, *Review of Central Government Control over Local Authorities* (1979) and the author's *Education and the Community* (1975).

A number of books and reports contribute to the debate about the state's relationship with schools. Prominent among these are G. H. Bantock, *Freedom and Authority in Education* (1952); J. Dewey, *The School and Society* (1900) or *Democracy and Education* (1916); M. Blaug, *Education: A Framework for Choice* (1970); HMSO, *A New Partnership for Schools*, The Taylor Report (1977); F. Musgrove, *The Family, Education and Society* (1966) and A. Seldon, *Charge* (1977).

Some students might wish to pursue in more depth the contribution of particular heroes—or villains—of our island's educational heritage, and here (ed) A. V. Judges, *Pioneers of English Education* (1952) provides an excellent starting point. Then there is B. M. Allen, *Sir Robert Morant* (1934); W. F. Connell, *The Educational Thought and Influence of Matthew Arnold* (1950); R. Lowe, *Middle-class Education: Endowment or Free Trade* (1868); T. Wemyss-Reid, *Life of W. E. Forster* (1888) and R. J. Halliday, *John Stuart Mill* (1976).

This section ended with a brief examination of teaching and teacher-training. Supportive reading may be found in R. Bourne and B. Macarthur, *The Struggle for Education, 1870-1970* (1970); P. H. J. H. Gosden, *The Evolution of a Profession* (1972); A Tropp, *The School Teacher: The Growth of the Teaching in England and Wales from 1800 to the Present Day* (1957); L. J. Westwood, *Teachers: Their Role in School and Society* (1969); D. Hencke, *The College in Crisis* (1978); R. W. Rich, *The Training of Teachers in England and*

Wales during the Nineteenth Century (1935); HMSO *Teacher Education and Training*, The James Report, (1972); and N. A. Flanders *Analysing Teaching Behaviour* (1970).

EDUCATION AND THE SCHOOLS

An excellent base for this section would be E. J. R. Eaglesham, *The Foundations of Twentieth Century Education in England* (1967), while, for those needing a prelude to this, F. Smith, *A History of English Elementary Education, 1760-1902* (1931) might be helpful.

For pre-school and primary school reading, W. A. L. Blyth, *English Primary Education* (1965); HMSO, *Children and their Primary Schools*, The Plowden Report (1967); R. R. Rush, *A History of Infant Education* (1933); HMSO, *Primary Education in England* (1978); B. Tizzard, *Pre-school Education in Great Britain* (1974) and G. A. Poulton and T. James *Pre-school Learning in the Community* (1975) are all heartily recommended.

For secondary school reading, R. L. Archer, *Secondary Education in the Nineteenth Century* (1932) for the build-up. C. Benn and B. Simon, *Halfway There* (1970) for the recent past, and M. Rutter, *Fifteen Thousand Hours* (1979) for the present, and, one hopes, the future, are suggested. There is also H. Ree *Educator Extraordinary: The Life and Achievement of Henry Morris* (1973); C. Ward and A. Fyson *Streetwork: The Exploding School* (1973).

For aspects of post-school education touched on in the last two or three chapters, one might turn to M. Newman, *The Poor Cousin; a Study of Adult Education*; R. Pedley, *The Comprehensive University* (1978); HMSO *Adult Education: A Plan for Development*, The Russell Report (1973); (ed) V. Houghton and K. Richardson, *Recurrent Education* (1974); T. Lovett, *Adult Education, Community Development and the Working Class* (1975) and the author's *Patterns of Community Education* (1973).

There are, of course, scores of books on the several issues necessarily alluded to throughout the text. There follows an unavoidably arbitrary selection of books which should prove of assistance to those wishing to pursue special themes. D. Lawton, *Social Change, Educational Theory and Curriculum Planning* (1973); M. Kellmer Pringle *et al. Eleven Thousand Seven Year Olds* (1966); D. Salmon, *Lancaster's Improvements and Bell's Experiments* (1932); D. H. Cohen, *The Learning Child* (1973); N. Garner *et al. Teaching in the Urban Community School* (1973); (ed) R. Hooper, *The Curriculum; Content, Design and Development* (1971); (ed) T. Roberts, *The Circumstances of Learning* (1976); (ed) B. Crick and A. Porter, *Political Education and Political Literacy* (1978) and the author's *Education for Sale* (1976).

This is far from being an exclusive list; some may feel it verges rather on the idiosyncratic. It is essentially a log of those books and reports which, it is personally believed, would provide the most illuminating reading, granted the themes that have been discussed in the text and the pattern of argument that has been pursued. Certainly a hundred publications have been mentioned, and few would doubt that a perusal of this century of books would be of substantial benefit to the student who wished to understand more completely and clearly the problems and challenges of English education over the next decades.

INDEX

This book is arranged thematically, as outlined in the Introduction (p 8). There are also cross-references to other chapters as appropriate in the text, and many of the authors referred to are included in detail in the Further Reading section, (pp. 181-185). The index is chiefly related, therefore, to the names of contributors to the debate about and the practice of English education; places (mainly local authority or similar areas) and organizations.